KAHLIL GIBRAN
Popular Works

KAHLIL GIBRAN
Popular Works

- The Prophet
- The Madman
- The Forerunner
- Prose Poems

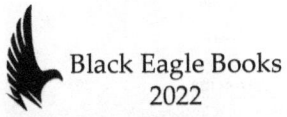

Black Eagle Books
2022

Black Eagle Books
USA address:
7464 Wisdom Lane
Dublin, OH 43016

India address:
E/312, Trident Galaxy, Kalinga Nagar,
Bhubaneswar-751003, Odisha, India

E-mail: info@blackeaglebooks.org
Website: www.blackeaglebooks.org

First International Edition Published by
Black Eagle Books, 2022

KAHLIL GIBRAN POPULAR WORKS
(The Prophet, The Madman, The Forerunner & Prose Poems)
by **KAHLIL GIBRAN**

Copyright © BEB

All rights reserved. No part of this publication may be reproduced, stored in a retrieval system, or transmitted, in any form or by any means, electronic, mechanical, photocopying, recording or otherwise without the prior permission of the publisher.

Cover & Interior Design: Ezy's Publication

ISBN- 978-1-64560-300-9 (Paperback)

Printed in the United States of America

Contents

THE PROPHET

The Coming of the Ship	11
On Love	17
On Marriage	20
On Children	22
On Giving	24
On Eating and Drinking	27
On Work	29
On Joy and Sorrow	32
On Houses	33
On Clothes	35
On Buying and Selling	36
On Crime and Punishment	39
On Laws	42
On Freedom	44
On Reason and Passion	46
On Pain	48
On Self-Knowledge	50
On Teaching	51
On Friendship	52
On Talking	54
On Time	56
On Good and Evil	57
On Prayer	59
On Pleasure	62
On Beauty	65
On Religion	67
On Death	69
The Farewell	72

THE MADMAN

God	86
My friend	87
The scarecrow	89
The sleep-walkers	90
The wise dog	91
The two hermits	92
On giving and taking	93
The seven selves	94
War	96
The fox	98
The wise king	99
Ambition	100
The new pleasure	101
The other language	102
The pomegranate	104
The two cages	105
The three ants	106
The grave-digger	107
On the steps of the temple	108
The blessed city	109
The good god and the evil god	111
Defeat	112
Night and the madman	113
Faces	116
The greater sea	117
Crucified	119
The astronomer	120
The great longing	121
Said a blade of grass	122
The eye	123
The two learned men	124
When my sorrow was born	125
And when my joy was born	126
The perfect world	127

THE FORERUNNER

God's fool	133
Love	136
The king-hermit	137
The lion's daughter	141
Tyranny	143
The saint	144
The plutocrat	146
The greater self	147
War and the small nations	149
Critics	151
Poets	152
The weather-cock	153
The king of aradus	154
Out of my deeper heart	155
Dynasties	156
Knowledge and half-knowledge	158
"Said a sheet of snow-white paper...."	160
The scholar and the poet	161
Values	163
Other seas	164
Repentance	165
The dying man and the vulture	166
Beyond my solitude	169
The last watch	170

PROSE POEMS

At the door of the temple	177
Revelation	183
The soul	186
Song of the night	189
My soul counselled me	191
My birthday	197
Be still, my heart	206
Night	217
In the city of the dead	223
The poet	228
Fame	233
Earth	234

THE PROPHET

The Coming of the Ship

Almustafa, the chosen and the beloved, who was a dawn unto his own day, had waited twelve years in the city of Orphalese for his ship that was to return and bear him back to the isle of his birth.

And in the twelfth year, on the seventh day of Ielool, the month of reaping, he climbed the hill without the city walls and looked seaward; and he beheld his ship coming with the mist.

Then the gates of his heart were flung open, and his joy flew far over the sea. And he closed his eyes and prayed in the silences of his soul.

But as he descended the hill, a sadness came upon him, and he thought in his heart:

How shall I go in peace and without sorrow? Nay, not without a wound in the spirit shall I leave this city.

Long were the days of pain I have spent within its walls, and long were the nights of aloneness; and who can depart from his pain and his aloneness without regret?

Too many fragments of the spirit have I scattered in these streets, and too many are the children of my longing that walk naked among these hills, and I cannot withdraw from them without a burden and an ache.

It is not a garment I cast off this day, but a skin that I tear with my own hands.

Nor is it a thought I leave behind me, but a heart made sweet with hunger and with thirst.

Yet I cannot tarry longer.

The sea that calls all things unto her calls me, and I must embark.

For to stay, though the hours burn in the night, is to freeze and crystallize and be bound in a mould.

Fain would I take with me all that is here. But how shall I?

A voice cannot carry the tongue and the lips that gave it wings. Alone must it seek the ether.

And alone and without his nest shall the eagle fly across the sun.

Now when he reached the foot of the hill, he turned again towards the sea, and he saw his ship approaching the harbour, and upon her prow the mariners, the men of his own land.

And his soul cried out to them, and he said:

Sons of my ancient mother, you riders of the tides,

How often have you sailed in my dreams. And now you come in my awakening, which is my deeper dream.

Ready am I to go, and my eagerness with sails full set awaits the wind.

Only another breath will I breathe in this still air, only another loving look cast backward,

And then I shall stand among you, a seafarer among seafarers.

And you, vast sea, sleepless mother,

Who alone are peace and freedom to the river and the stream,

Only another winding will this stream make, only another murmur in this glade,

And then shall I come to you, a boundless drop to a boundless ocean.

And as he walked he saw from afar men and women

leaving their fields and their vineyards and hastening towards the city gates.

And he heard their voices calling his name, and shouting from field to field telling one another of the coming of his ship.

And he said to himself:

Shall the day of parting be the day of gathering?

And shall it be said that my eve was in truth my dawn?

And what shall I give unto him who has left his plough in midfurrow, or to him who has stopped the wheel of his winepress?

Shall my heart become a tree heavy-laden with fruit that I may gather and give unto them?

And shall my desires flow like a fountain that I may fill their cups?

Am I a harp that the hand of the mighty may touch me, or a flute that his breath may pass through me?

A seeker of silences am I, and what treasure have I found in silences that I may dispense with confidence?

If this is my day of harvest, in what fields have I sowed the seed, and in what unremembered seasons?

If this indeed be the hour in which I lift up my lantern, it is not my flame that shall burn therein.

Empty and dark shall I raise my lantern,

And the guardian of the night shall fill it with oil and he shall light it also.

These things he said in words. But much in his heart remained unsaid. For he himself could not speak his deeper secret.

And when he entered into the city all the people came to meet him, and they were crying out to him as with one voice.

And the elders of the city stood forth and said:
Go not yet away from us.

A noontide have you been in our twilight, and your youth has given us dreams to dream.

No stranger are you among us, nor a guest, but our son and our dearly beloved.

Suffer not yet our eyes to hunger for your face.

And the priests and the priestesses said unto him:
Let not the waves of the sea separate us now, and the years you have spent in our midst become a memory.

You have walked among us a spirit, and your shadow has been a light upon our faces.

Much have we loved you. But speechless was our love, and with veils has it been veiled.

Yet now it cries aloud unto you, and would stand revealed before you.

And ever has it been that love knows not its own depth until the hour of separation.

And others came also and entreated him. But he answered them not. He only bent his head; and those who stood near saw his tears falling upon his breast.

And he and the people proceeded towards the great square before the temple.

And there came out of the sanctuary a woman whose name was Almitra. And she was a seeress.

And he looked upon her with exceeding tenderness, for it was she who had first sought and believed in him when he had been but a day in their city.

And she hailed him, saying:
Prophet of God, in quest of the uttermost, long have you searched the distances for your ship.

And now your ship has come, and you must needs go.

Deep is your longing for the land of your memories

and the dwelling place of your greater desires; and our love would not bind you nor our needs hold you.

Yet this we ask ere you leave us, that you speak to us and give us of your truth.

And we will give it unto our children, and they unto their children, and it shall not perish.

In your aloneness you have watched with our days, and in your wakefulness you have listened to the weeping and the laughter of our sleep.

Now therefore disclose us to ourselves, and tell us all that has been shown you of that which is between birth and death.

And he answered,

People of Orphalese, of what can I speak save of that which is even now moving within your souls?

On Love

Then said Almitra, Speak to us of Love.
And he raised his head and looked upon the people, and there fell a stillness upon them. And with a great voice he said:

When love beckons to you, follow him,
Though his ways are hard and steep.
And when his wings enfold you yield to him,
Though the sword hidden among his pinions may wound you.
And when he speaks to you believe in him,
Though his voice may shatter your dreams as the north wind lays waste the garden.

For even as love crowns you so shall he crucify you. Even as he is for your growth so is he for your pruning.
Even as he ascends to your height and caresses your tenderest branches that quiver in the sun,
So shall he descend to your roots and shake them in their clinging to the earth.
Like sheaves of corn he gathers you unto himself.
He threshes you to make you naked.
He sifts you to free you from your husks.
He grinds you to whiteness.
He kneads you until you are pliant;
And then he assigns you to his sacred fire, that you may become sacred bread for God's sacred feast.

All these things shall love do unto you that you may know the secrets of your heart, and in that knowledge become a fragment of Life's heart.

But if in your fear you would seek only love's peace and love's pleasure,

Then it is better for you that you cover your nakedness and pass out of love's threshing-floor,

Into the seasonless world where you shall laugh, but not all of your laughter, and weep, but not all of your tears.

Love gives naught but itself and takes naught but from itself.

Love possesses not nor would it be possessed;

For love is sufficient unto love.

When you love you should not say, "God is in my heart," but rather, "I am in the heart of God."

And think not you can direct the course of love, for love, if it finds you worthy, directs your course.

Love has no other desire but to fulfil itself.

But if you love and must needs have desires, let these be your desires:

To melt and be like a running brook that sings its melody to the night.

To know the pain of too much tenderness.

To be wounded by your own understanding of love;

And to bleed willingly and joyfully.

To wake at dawn with a winged heart and give thanks for another day of loving;

To rest at the noon hour and meditate love's ecstacy;

To return home at eventide with gratitude;

And then to sleep with a prayer for the beloved in your heart and a song of praise upon your lips.

On Marriage

Then Almitra spoke again and said, And what of Marriage master?

And he answered saying:

You were born together, and together you shall be forevermore.

You shall be together when the white wings of death scatter your days.

Aye, you shall be together even in the silent memory of God.

But let there be spaces in your togetherness,

And let the winds of the heavens dance between you.

Love one another, but make not a bond of love:

Let it rather be a moving sea between the shores of your souls.

Fill each other's cup but drink not from one cup.

Give one another of your bread but eat not from the same loaf.

Sing and dance together and be joyous, but let each one of you be alone,

Even as the strings of a lute are alone though they quiver with the same music.

Give your hearts, but not into each other's keeping.

For only the hand of Life can contain your hearts.

And stand together yet not too near together:

For the pillars of the temple stand apart,

And the oak tree and the cypress grow not in each other's shadow.

On Children

And a woman who held a babe against her bosom said, Speak to us of Children.

And he said:

Your children are not your children.

They are the sons and daughters of Life's longing for itself.

They come through you but not from you,

And though they are with you yet they belong not to you.

You may give them your love but not your thoughts,

For they have their own thoughts.

You may house their bodies but not their souls,

For their souls dwell in the house of tomorrow, which you cannot visit, not even in your dreams.

You may strive to be like them, but seek not to make them like you.

For life goes not backward nor tarries with yesterday.

You are the bows from which your children as living arrows are sent forth.

The archer sees the mark upon the path of the infinite, and He bends you with His might that His arrows may go swift and far.

Let your bending in the Archer's hand be for gladness;

For even as he loves the arrow that flies, so He loves also the bow that is stable.

On Giving

Then said a rich man, Speak to us of Giving.
And he answered:

You give but little when you give of your possessions.

It is when you give of yourself that you truly give.

For what are your possessions but things you keep and guard for fear you may need them tomorrow?

And tomorrow, what shall tomorrow bring to the overprudent dog burying bones in the trackless sand as he follows the pilgrims to the holy city?

And what is fear of need but need itself?

Is not dread of thirst when your well is full, the thirst that is unquenchable?

There are those who give little of the much which they have--and they give it for recognition and their hidden desire makes their gifts unwholesome.

And there are those who have little and give it all.

These are the believers in life and the bounty of life, and their coffer is never empty.

There are those who give with joy, and that joy is their reward.

And there are those who give with pain, and that pain is their baptism.

And there are those who give and know not pain in giving, nor do they seek joy, nor give with mindfulness of virtue;

They give as in yonder valley the myrtle breathes its fragrance into space.

Through the hands of such as these God speaks, and from behind their eyes He smiles upon the earth.

It is well to give when asked, but it is better to give unasked, through understanding;

And to the open-handed the search for one who shall receive is joy greater than giving.

And is there aught you would withhold?

All you have shall some day be given;

Therefore give now, that the season of giving may be yours and not your inheritors'.

You often say, "I would give, but only to the deserving."

The trees in your orchard say not so, nor the flocks in your pasture.

They give that they may live, for to withhold is to perish.

Surely he who is worthy to receive his days and his nights, is worthy of all else from you.

And he who has deserved to drink from the ocean of life deserves to fill his cup from your little stream.

And what desert greater shall there be, than that which lies in the courage and the confidence, nay the charity, of receiving?

And who are you that men should rend their bosom and unveil their pride, that you may see their worth naked and their pride unabashed?

See first that you yourself deserve to be a giver, and an instrument of giving.

For in truth it is life that gives unto life--while you, who deem yourself a giver, are but a witness.

And you receivers--and you are all receivers--assume no weight of gratitude, lest you lay a yoke upon yourself and upon him who gives.

Rather rise together with the giver on his gifts as on wings;

For to be overmindful of your debt, is ito doubt his generosity who has the freehearted earth for mother, and God for father.

On Eating and Drinking

Then an old man, a keeper of an inn, said, Speak to us of Eating and Drinking.

And he said:

Would that you could live on the fragrance of the earth, and like an air plant be sustained by the light.

But since you must kill to eat, and rob the newly born of its mother's milk to quench your thirst, let it then be an act of worship,

And let your board stand an altar on which the pure and the innocent of forest and plain are sacrificed for that which is purer and still more innocent in man.

When you kill a beast say to him in your heart,

"By the same power that slays you, I too am slain; and I too shall be consumed.

For the law that delivered you into my hand shall deliver me into a mightier hand.

Your blood and my blood is naught but the sap that feeds the tree of heaven."

And when you crush an apple with your teeth, say to it in your heart,

"Your seeds shall live in my body,

And the buds of your tomorrow shall blossom in my heart,

And your fragrance shall be my breath, And together we shall rejoice through all the seasons."

And in the autumn, when you gather the grapes of your vineyards for the winepress, say in your heart,

"I too am a vineyard, and my fruit shall be gathered for the winepress,

And like new wine I shall be kept in eternal vessels."

And in winter, when you draw the wine, let there be in your heart a song for each cup;

And let there be in the song a remembrance for the autumn days, and for the vineyard, and for the winepress.

On Work

Then a ploughman said, Speak to us of Work.
And he answered, saying:
You work that you may keep pace with the earth and the soul of the earth.

For to be idle is to become a stranger unto the seasons, and to step out of life's procession, that marches in majesty and proud submission towards the infinite.

When you work you are a flute through whose heart the whispering of the hours turns to music.

Which of you would be a reed, dumb and silent, when all else sings together in unison?

Always you have been told that work is a curse and labour a misfortune.

But I say to you that when you work you fulfil a part of earth's furthest dream, assigned to you when that dream was born,

And in keeping yourself with labour you are in truth loving life,

And to love life through labour is to be intimate with life's inmost secret.

But if you in your pain call birth an affliction and the support of the flesh a curse written upon your brow, then I answer that naught but the sweat of your brow shall wash away that which is written.

You have been told also that life is darkness, and in your weariness you echo what was said by the weary.

And I say that life is indeed darkness 'save when there is urge,

And all urge is blind save when there is knowledge,

And all knowledge is vain save when there is work,

And all work is empty save when there is love;

And when you work with love you bind yourself to yourself, and to one another, and to God.

And what is it to work with love?

It is to weave the cloth with threads drawn from your heart, even as if your beloved were to wear that cloth.

It is to build a house with affection, even as if your beloved were to dwell in that house.

It is to sow seeds with tenderness and reap the harvest with joy, even as if your beloved were to eat the fruit.

It is to charge all things you fashion with a breath of your own spirit,

And to know that all the blessed dead are standing about you and watching.

Often have I heard you say, as if speaking in sleep, "He who works in marble, and finds the shape of his own soul in the stone, is nobler than he who ploughs the soil.

And he who seizes the rainbow to lay it on a cloth in the likeness of man, is more than he who makes the sandals for our feet."

But I say, not in sleep but in the overwakefulness of noontide, that the wind speaks not more sweetly to the giant oaks than to the least of all the blades of grass;

And he alone is great who turns the voice of the wind into a song made sweeter by his own loving.

Work is love made visible.

And if you cannot work with love but only with distaste, it is better that you should leave your work and sit at the gate of the temple and take alms of those who work with joy.

For if you bake bread with indifference, you bake a bitter bread that feeds but half man's hunger.

And if you grudge the crushing of the grapes, your grudge distils a poison in the wine.

And if you sing though as angels, and love not the singing, you muffle man's ears to the voices of the day and the voices of the night.

On Joy and Sorrow

Then a woman said, Speak to us of Joy and Sorrow.
And he answered:

Your joy is your sorrow unmasked.

And the selfsame well from which your laughter rises was oftentimes filled with your tears.

And how else can it be?

The deeper that sorrow carves into your being, the more joy you can contain.

Is not the cup that holds your wine the very cup that was burned in the potter's oven?

And is not the lute that soothes your spirit, the very wood that was hollowed with knives?

When you are joyous, look deep into your heart and you shall find it is only that which has given you sorrow that is giving you joy.

When you are sorrowful look again in your heart, and you shall see that in truth you are weeping for that which has been your delight.

Some of you say, "Joy is greater than sorrow," and others say, "Nay, sorrow is the greater."

But I say unto you, they are inseparable.

Together they come, and when one sits alone with you at your board, remember that the other is asleep upon your bed.

Verily you are suspended like scales between your sorrow and your joy.

Only when you are empty are you at standstill and balanced.

When the treasure-keeper lifts you to weigh his gold and his silver, needs must your joy or your sorrow rise or fall.

On Houses

Then a mason came forth and said, Speak to us of Houses. And he answered and said:

Build of your imaginings a bower in the wilderness ere you build a house within the city walls.

For even as you have home-comings in your twilight, so has the wanderer in you, the ever distant and alone.

Your house is your larger body.

It grows in the sun and sleeps in the stillness of the night; and it is not dreamless. Does not your house dream? and dreaming, leave the city for grove or hilltop?

Would that I could gather your houses into my hand, and like a sower scatter them in forest and meadow.

Would the valleys were your streets, and the green paths your alleys, that you might seek one another through vineyards, and come with the fragrance of the earth in your garments.

But these things are not yet to be.

In their fear your forefathers gathered you too near together. And that fear shall endure a little longer. A little longer shall your city walls separate your hearths from your fields.

And tell me, people of Orphalese, what have you in these houses? And what is it you guard with fastened doors?

Have you peace, the quiet urge that reveals your power?

Have you remembrances, the glimmering arches that span the summits of the mind?

Have you beauty, that leads the heart from things fashioned of wood and stone to the holy mountain?

Tell me, have you these in your houses?

Or have you only comfort, and the lust for comfort, that stealthy thing that enters the house a guest, and then becomes a host, and then a master?

Ay, and it becomes a tamer, and with hook and scourge makes puppets of your larger desires.

Though its hands are silken, its heart is of iron.

It lulls you to sleep only to stand by your bed and jeer at the dignity of the flesh.

It makes mock of your sound senses, and lays them in thistledown like fragile vessels.

Verily the lust for comfort murders the passion of the soul, and then walks grinning in the funeral.

But you, children of space, you restless in rest, you shall not be trapped nor tamed.

Your house shall be not an anchor but a mast.

It shall not be a glistening film that covers a wound, but an eyelid that guards the eye.

You shall not fold your wings that you may pass through doors, nor bend your heads that they strike not against a ceiling, nor fear to breathe lest walls should crack and fall down.

You shall not dwell in tombs made by the dead for the living.

And though of magnificence and splendour, your house shall not hold your secret nor shelter your longing.

For that which is boundless in you abides in the mansion of the sky, whose door is the morning mist, and whose windows are the songs and the silences of night.

On Clothes

And the weaver said, Speak to us of Clothes.
And he answered:

Your clothes conceal much of your beauty, yet they hide not the unbeautiful.

And though you seek in garments the freedom of privacy you may find in them a harness and a chain.

Would that you could meet the sun and the wind with more of your skin and less of your raiment,

For the breath of life is in the sunlight and the hand of life is in the wind.

Some of you say, "It is the north wind who has woven the clothes we wear."

And I say, Ay, it was the north wind,

But shame was his loom, and the softening of the sinews was his thread.

And when his work was done he laughed in the forest.

Forget not that modesty is for a shield against the eye of the unclean.

And when the unclean shall be no more, what were modesty but a fetter and a fouling of the mind?

And forget not that the earth delights to feel your bare feet and the winds long to play with your hair.

On Buying and Selling

And a merchant said, Speak to us of Buying and Selling. And he answered and said:

To you the earth yields her fruit, and you shall not want if you but know how to fill your hands.

It is in exchanging the gifts of the earth that you shall find abundance and be satisfied.

Yet unless the exchange be in love and kindly justice, it will but lead some to greed and others to hunger.

When in the market place you toilers of the sea and fields and vineyards meet the weavers and the potters and the gatherers of spices,--

Invoke then the master spirit of the earth, to come into your midst and sanctify the scales and the reckoning that weighs value against value.

And suffer not the barren-handed to take part in your transactions, who would sell their words for your labour.

To such men you should say,

"Come with us to the field, or go with our brothers to the sea and cast your net;

For the land and the sea shall be bountiful to you even as to us."

And if there come the singers and the dancers and the flute players,--buy of their gifts also.

For they too are gatherers of fruit and frankincense, and that which they bring, though fashioned of dreams, is raiment and food for your soul.

And before you leave the market place, see that no one has gone his way with empty hands.

For the master spirit of the earth shall not sleep peacefully upon the wind till the needs of the least of you are satisfied.

On Crime and Punishment

Then one of the judges of the city stood forth and said, Speak to us of Crime and Punishment.

And he answered, saying:

It is when your spirit goes wandering upon the wind,

That you, alone and unguarded, commit a wrong unto others and therefore unto yourself.

And for that wrong committed must you knock and wait a while unheeded at the gate of the blessed.

Like the ocean is your god-self;

It remains for ever undefiled.

And like the ether it lifts but the winged.

Even like the sun is your god-self;

It knows not the ways of the mole nor seeks it the holes of the serpent.

But your god-self dwells not alone in your being.

Much in you is still man, and much in you is not yet man,

But a shapeless pigmy that walks asleep in the mist searching for its own awakening.

And of the man in you would I now speak.

For it is he and not your god-self nor the pigmy in the mist, that knows crime and the punishment of crime.

Oftentimes have I heard you speak of one who commits a wrong as though he were not one of you, but a stranger unto you and an intruder upon your world.

But I say that even as the holy and the righteous cannot rise beyond the highest which is in each one of you,

So the wicked and the weak cannot fall lower than the lowest which is in you also.

And as a single leaf turns not yellow but with the silent knowledge of the whole tree,

So the wrong-doer cannot do wrong without the hidden will of you all.

Like a procession you walk together towards your god-self.

You are the way and the wayfarers.

And when one of you falls down he falls for those behind him, a caution against the stumbling stone.

Ay, and he falls for those ahead of him, who though faster and surer of foot, yet removed not the stumbling stone.

And this also, though the word lie heavy upon your hearts:

The murdered is not unaccountable for his own murder,

And the robbed is not blameless in being robbed.

The righteous is not innocent of the deeds of the wicked,

And the white-handed is not clean in the doings of the felon.

Yea, the guilty is oftentimes the victim of the injured,

And still more often the condemned is the burden bearer for the guiltless and unblamed.

You cannot separate the just from the unjust and the good from the wicked;

For they stand together before the face of the sun even as the black thread and the white are woven together.

And when the black thread breaks, the weaver shall look into the whole cloth, and he shall examine the loom also.

If any of you would bring to judgment the unfaithful wife,

Let him also weigh the heart of her husband in scales, and measure his soul with measurements.

And let him who would lash the offender look unto the spirit of the offended.

And if any of you would punish in the name of righteousness and lay the ax unto the evil tree, let him see to its roots;

And verily he will find the roots of the good and the bad, the fruitful and the fruitless, all entwined together in the silent heart of the earth.

And you judges who would be just,

What judgment pronounce you upon him who though honest in the flesh yet is a thief in spirit?

What penalty lay you upon him who slays in the flesh yet is himself slain in the spirit?

And how prosecute you him who in action is a deceiver and an oppressor,

Yet who also is aggrieved and outraged?

And how shall you punish those whose remorse is already greater than their misdeeds?

Is not remorse the justice which is administered by that very law which you would fain serve?

Yet you cannot lay remorse upon the innocent nor lift it from the heart of the guilty.

Unbidden shall it call in the night, that men may wake and gaze upon themselves.

And you who would understand justice, how shall you unless you look upon all deeds in the fullness of light?

Only then shall you know that the erect and the fallen are but one man standing in twilight between the night of his pigmy-self and the day of his god-self, And that the corner-stone of the temple is not higher than the lowest stone in its foundation.

On Laws

Then a lawyer said, But what of our Laws, master? And he answered:

You delight in laying down laws,

Yet you delight more in breaking them.

Like children playing by the ocean who build sand-towers with constancy and then destroy them with laughter.

But while you build your sand-towers the ocean brings more sand to the shore,

And when you destroy them the ocean laughs with you.

Verily the ocean laughs always with the innocent.

But what of those to whom life is not an ocean, and man-made laws are not sand-towers,

But to whom life is a rock, and the law a chisel with which they would carve it in their own likeness?

What of the cripple who hates dancers?

What of the ox who loves his yoke and deems the elk and deer of the forest stray and vagrant things?

What of the old serpent who cannot shed his skin, and calls all others naked and shameless?

And of him who comes early to the wedding-feast, and when over-fed and tired goes his way saying that all feasts are violation and all feasters lawbreakers?

What shall I say of these save that they too stand in the sunlight, but with their backs to the sun?

They see only their shadows, and their shadows are their laws.

And what is the sun to them but a caster of shadows?

And what is it to acknowledge the laws but to stoop down and trace their shadows upon the earth?

But you who walk facing the sun, what images drawn on the earth can hold you?

You who travel with the wind, what weather-vane shall direct your course?

What man's law shall bind you if you break your yoke but upon no man's prison door?

What laws shall you fear if you dance but stumble against no man's iron chains?

And who is he that shall bring you to judgment if you tear off your garment yet leave it in no man's path?

People of Orphalese, you can muffle the drum, and you can loosen the strings of the lyre, but who shall command the skylark not to sing?

On Freedom

And an orator said, Speak to us of Freedom.
And he answered:

At the city gate and by your fireside I have seen you prostrate yourself and worship your own freedom,

Even as slaves humble themselves before a tyrant and praise him though he slays them.

Ay, in the grove of the temple and in the shadow of the citadel I have seen the freest among you wear their freedom as a yoke and a handcuff.

And my heart bled within me; for you can only be free when even the desire of seeking freedom becomes a harness to you, and when you cease to speak of freedom as a goal and a fulfilment.

You shall be free indeed when your days are not without a care nor your nights without a want and a grief,

But rather when these things girdle your life and yet you rise above them naked and unbound.

And how shall you rise beyond your days and nights unless you break the chains which you at the dawn of your understanding have fastened around your noon hour?

In truth that which you call freedom is the strongest of these chains, though its links glitter in the sun and dazzle your eyes.

And what is it but fragments of your own self you would discard that you may become free?

If it is an unjust law you would abolish, that law was written with your own hand upon your own forehead.

You cannot erase it by burning your law books nor by washing the foreheads of your judges, though you pour the sea upon them.

And if it is a despot you would dethrone, see first that his throne erected within you is destroyed.

For how can a tyrant rule the free and the proud, but for a tyranny in their own freedom and a shame in their own pride?

And if it is a care you would cast off, that cart has been chosen by you rather than imposed upon you.

And if it is a fear you would dispel, the seat of that fear is in your heart and not in the hand of the feared.

Verily all things move within your being in constant half embrace, the desired and the dreaded, the repugnant and the cherished, the pursued and that which you would escape.

These things move within you as lights and shadows in pairs that cling.

And when the shadow fades and is no more, the light that lingers becomes a shadow to another light.

And thus your freedom when it loses its fetters becomes itself the fetter of a greater freedom.

On Reason and Passion

And the priestess spoke again and said: Speak to us of Reason and Passion.

And he answered, saying:

Your soul is oftentimes a battlefield, upon which your reason and your judgment wage war against your passion and your appetite.

Would that I could be the peacemaker in your soul, that I might turn the discord and the rivalry of your elements into oneness and melody.

But how shall I, unless you yourselves be also the peacemakers, nay, the lovers of all your elements?

Your reason and your passion are the rudder and the sails of your seafaring soul.

If either your sails or your rudder be broken, you can but toss and drift, or else be held at a standstill in mid-seas.

For reason, ruling alone, is a force confining; and passion, unattended, is a flame that burns to its own destruction.

Therefore let your soul exalt your reason to the height of passion, that it may sing;

And let it direct your passion with reason, that your passion may live through its own daily resurrection, and like the phoenix rise above its own ashes.

I would have you consider your judgment and your appetite even as you would two loved guests in your house.

Surely you would not honour one guest above the other; for he who is more mindful of one loses the love and the faith of both

Among the hills, when you sit in the cool shade of the white poplars, sharing the peace and serenity of distant fields and meadows--then let your heart say in silence, "God rests in reason."

And when the storm comes, and the mighty wind shakes the forest, and thunder and lightning proclaim the majesty of the sky,--then let your heart say in awe, "God moves in passion."

And since you are a breath in God's sphere, and a leaf in God's forest, you too should rest in reason and move in passion.

On Pain

And a woman spoke, saying, Tell us of Pain.
And he said:
Your pain is the breaking of the shell that encloses your understanding.

Even as the stone of the fruit must break, that its heart may stand in the sun, so must you know pain.

And could you keep your heart in wonder at the daily miracles of your life, your pain would not seem less wondrous than your joy;

And you would accept the seasons of your heart, even as you have always accepted the seasons that pass over your fields.

And you would watch with serenity through the winters of your grief.

Much of your pain is self-chosen.

It is the bitter potion by which the physician within you heals your sick self.

Therefore trust the physician, and drink his remedy in silence and tranquillity: For his hand, though heavy and hard, is guided by the tender hand of the Unseen, And the cup he brings, though it burn your lips, has been fashioned of the clay which the Potter has moistened with His own sacred tears.

On Self-Knowledge

And a man said, Speak to us of Self-Knowledge.
And he answered, saying:
Your hearts know in silence the secrets of the days and the nights.
But your ears thirst for the sound of your heart's knowledge.
You would know in words that which you have always known in thought.
You would touch with your fingers the naked body of your dreams.
And it is well you should.
The hidden well-spring of your soul must needs rise and run murmuring to the sea;
And the treasure of your infinite depths would be revealed to your eyes.
But let there be no scales to weigh your unknown treasure; And seek not the depths of your knowledge with staff or sounding line.
For self is a sea boundless and measureless.
Say not, "I have found the truth," but rather, "I have found a truth."
Say not, "I have found the path of the soul." Say rather, "I have met the soul walking upon my path."
For the soul walks upon all paths.
The soul walks not upon a line, neither does it grow like a reed.
The soul unfolds itself, like a lotus of countless petals.

On Teaching

Then said a teacher, Speak to us of Teaching.
And he said:
"No man can reveal to you aught but that which already lies half asleep in the dawning of your knowledge.

The teacher who walks in the shadow of the temple, among his followers, gives not of his wisdom but rather of his faith and his lovingness.

If he is indeed wise he does not bid you enter the house of his wisdom, but rather leads you to the threshold of your own mind.

The astronomer may speak to you of his understanding of space, but he cannot give you his understanding.

The musician may sing to you of the rhythm which is in all space, but he cannot give you the ear which arrests the rhythm nor the voice that echoes it.

And he who is versed in the science of numbers can tell of the regions of weight and measure, but he cannot conduct you thither.

For the vision of one man lends not its wings to another man.

And even as each one of you stands alone in God's knowledge, so must each one of you be alone in his knowledge of God and in his understanding of the earth.

On Friendship

And a youth said, Speak to us of Friendship.
And he answered, saying:
    Your friend is your needs answered.
    He is your field which you sow with love and reap with thanksgiving.
    And he is your board and your fireside.
    For you come to him with your hunger, and you seek him for peace.
    When your friend speaks his mind you fear not the "nay" in your own mind, nor do you withhold the "ay."
    And when he is silent your heart ceases not to listen to his heart;
    For without words, in friendship, all thoughts, all desires, all expectations are born and shared, with joy that is unacclaimed.
    When you part from your friend, you grieve not;
    For that which you love most in him may be clearer in his absence, as the mountain to the climber is clearer from the plain.
    And let there be no purpose in friendship save the deepening of the spirit.
    For love that seeks aught but the disclosure of its own mystery is not love but a net cast forth: and only the unprofitable is caught.
    And let your best be for your friend.
    If he must know the ebb of your tide, let him know its flood also.

For what is your friend that you should seek him with hours to kill?

Seek him always with hours to live.

For it is his to fill your need, but not your emptiness.

And in the sweetness of friendship let there be laughter, and sharing of pleasures.

For in the dew of little things the heart finds its morning and is refreshed.

On Talking

And then a scholar said, Speak of Talking.
And he answered, saying:
You talk when you cease to be at peace with your thoughts;
And when you can no longer dwell in the solitude of your heart you live in your lips, and sound is a diversion and a pastime.
And in much of your talking, thinking is half murdered.
For thought is a bird of space, that in a cage of words may indeed unfold its wings but cannot fly.
There are those among you who seek the talkative through fear of being alone.
The silence of aloneness reveals to their eyes their naked selves and they would escape.
And there are those who talk, and without knowledge or forethought reveal a truth which they themselves do not understand.
And there are those who have the truth within them, but they tell it not in words.
In the bosom of such as these the spirit dwells in rhythmic silence.
When you meet your friend on the roadside or in the market place, let the spirit in you move your lips and direct your tongue.
Let the voice within your voice speak to the ear of his ear;

For his soul will keep the truth of your heart as the taste of the wine is remembered
When the colour is forgotten and the vessel is no more.

On Time

And an astronomer said, Master, what of Time?
And he answered:

You would measure time the measureless and the immeasurable.

You would adjust your conduct and even direct the course of your spirit according to hours and seasons.

Of time you would make a stream upon whose bank you would sit and watch its flowing.

Yet the timeless in you is aware of life's timelessness,

And knows that yesterday is but today's memory and tomorrow is today's dream.

And that that which sings and contemplates in you is still dwelling within the bounds of that first moment which scattered the stars into space.

Who among you does not feel that his power to love is boundless?

And yet who does not feel that very love, though boundless, encompassed within the centre of his being, and moving not from love thought to love thought, nor from love deeds to other love deeds?

And is not time even as love is, undivided and spaceless?

But if in your thought you must measure time into seasons, let each season encircle all the other seasons,

And let today embrace the past with remembrance and the future with longing.

On Good and Evil

And one of the elders of the city said, Speak to us of Good and Evil.

And he answered:

Of the good in you I can speak, but not of the evil.

For what is evil but good tortured by its own hunger and thirst?

Verily when good is hungry it seeks food even in dark caves, and when it thirsts it drinks even of dead waters.

You are good when you are one with yourself.

Yet when you are not one with yourself you are not evil.

For a divided house is not a den of thieves; it is only a divided house.

And a ship without rudder may wander aimlessly among perilous isles yet sink not to the bottom.

You are good when you strive to give of yourself.

Yet you are not evil when you seek gain for yourself.

For when you strive for gain you are but a root that clings to the earth and sucks at her breast.

Surely the fruit cannot say to the root, "Be like me, ripe and full and ever giving of your abundance."

For to the fruit giving is a need, as receiving is a need to the root.

You are good when you are fully awake in your speech,

Yet you are not evil when you sleep while your tongue staggers without purpose.

And even stumbling speech may strengthen a weak tongue.

You are good when you walk to your goal firmly and with bold steps.

Yet you are not evil when you go thither limping.

Even those who limp go not backward.

But you who are strong and swift, see that you do not limp before the lame, deeming it kindness.

You are good in countless ways, and you are not evil when you are not good,

You are only loitering and sluggard.

Pity that the stags cannot teach swiftness to the turtles.

In your longing for your giant self lies your goodness: and that longing is in all of you.

But in some of you that longing is a torrent rushing with might to the sea, carrying the secrets of the hillsides and the songs of the forest.

And in others it is a flat stream that loses itself in angles and bends and lingers before it reaches the shore.

But let not him who longs much say to him who longs little, "Wherefore are you slow and halting?"

For the truly good ask not the naked, "Where is your garment?" nor the houseless, "What has befallen your house?"

On Prayer

Then a priestess said, Speak to us of Prayer.
And he answered, saying:
You pray in your distress and in your need; would that you might pray also in the fullness of your joy and in your days of abundance.

For what is prayer but the expansion of yourself into the living ether?

And if it is for your comfort to pour your darkness into space, it is also for your delight to pour forth the dawning of your heart.

And if you cannot but weep when your soul summons you to prayer, she should spur you again and yet again, though weeping, until you shall come laughing.

When you pray you rise to meet in the air those who are praying at that very hour, and whom save in prayer you may not meet.

Therefore let your visit to that temple invisible be for naught but ecstasy and sweet communion.

For if you should enter the temple for no other purpose than asking you shall not receive:

And if you should enter into it to humble yourself you shall not be lifted:

Or even if you should enter into it to beg for the good of others you shall not be heard.

It is enough that you enter the temple invisible.

I cannot teach you how to pray in words.

God listens not to your words save when He Himself utters them through your lips.

And I cannot teach you the prayer of the seas and the forests and the mountains.

But you who are born of the mountains and the forests and the seas can find their prayer in your heart,

And if you but listen in the stillness of the night you shall hear them saying in silence,

"Our God, who art our winged self, it is thy will in us that willeth.

It is thy desire in us that desireth.

It is thy urge in us that would turn our nights, which are thine, into days which are thine also.

We cannot ask thee for aught, for thou knowest our needs before they are born in us:

Thou art our need; and in giving us more of thyself thou givest us all."

On Pleasure

Then a hermit, who visited the city once a year, came forth and said, Speak to us of Pleasure.

And he answered, saying:

Pleasure is a freedom-song,

But it is not freedom.

It is the blossoming of your desires,

But it is not their fruit.

It is a depth calling unto a height,

But it is not the deep nor the high.

It is the caged taking wing,

But it is not space encompassed.

Ay, in very truth, pleasure is a freedom-song.

And I fain would have you sing it with fullness of heart; yet I would not have you lose your hearts in the singing.

Some of your youth seek pleasure as if it were all, and they are judged and rebuked.

I would not judge nor rebuke them. I would have them seek.

For they shall find pleasure, but not her alone;

Seven are her sisters, and the least of them is more beautiful than pleasure.

Have you not heard of the man who was digging in the earth for roots and found a treasure?

And some of your elders remember pleasures with regret like wrongs committed in drunkenness.

But regret is the beclouding of the mind and not its chastisement.

They should remember their pleasures with gratitude, as they would the harvest of a summer.

Yet if it comforts them to regret, let them be comforted.

And there are among you those who are neither young to seek nor old to remember;

And in their fear of seeking and remembering they shun all pleasures, lest they neglect the spirit or offend against it.

But even in their foregoing is their pleasure.

And thus they too find a treasure though they dig for roots with quivering hands.

But tell me, who is he that can offend the spirit?

Shall the nightingale offend the stillness of the night, or the firefly the stars?

And shall your flame or your smoke burden the wind?

Think you the spirit is a still pool which you can trouble with a staff?

Oftentimes in denying yourself pleasure you do but store the desire in the recesses of your being.

Who knows but that which seems omitted today, waits for tomorrow?

Even your body knows its heritage and its rightful need and will not be deceived.

And your body is the harp of your soul,

And it is yours to bring forth sweet music from it or confused sounds.

And now you ask in your heart, "How shall we distinguish that which is good in pleasure from that which is not good?"

Go to your fields and your gardens, and you shall learn that it is the pleasure of the bee to gather honey of the flower,

But it is also the pleasure of the flower to yield its honey to the bee.

For to the bee a flower is a fountain of life,

And to the flower a bee is a messenger of love,

And to both, bee and flower, the giving and the receiving of pleasure is a need and an ecstasy.

People of Orphalese, be in your pleasures like the flowers and the bees.

On Beauty

And a poet said, Speak to us of Beauty.
And he answered:

Where shall you seek beauty, and how shall you find her unless she herself be your way and your guide?

And how shall you speak of her except she be the weaver of your speech?

The aggrieved and the injured say, "Beauty is kind and gentle.

Like a young mother half-shy of her own glory she walks among us."

And the passionate say, "Nay, beauty is a thing of might and dread.

Like the tempest she shakes the earth beneath us and the sky above us."

The tired and the weary say, "Beauty is of soft whisperings. She speaks in our spirit.

Her voice yields to our silences like a faint light that quivers in fear of the shadow."

But the restless say, "We have heard her shouting among the mountains,

And with her cries came the sound of hoofs, and the beating of wings and the roaring of lions."

At night the watchmen of the city say, "Beauty shall rise with the dawn from the east."

And at noontide the toilers and the wayfarers say, "We have seen her leaning over the earth from the windows of the sunset."

In winter say the snow-bound, "She shall come with the spring leaping upon the hills."

And in the summer heat the reapers say, "We have seen her dancing with the autumn leaves, and we saw a drift of snow in her hair."

All these things have you said of beauty,

Yet in truth you spoke not of her but of needs unsatisfied,

And beauty is not a need but an ecstasy.

It is not a mouth thirsting nor an empty hand stretched forth,

But rather a heart enflamed and a soul enchanted.

It is not the image you would see nor the song you would hear,

But rather an image you see though you close your eyes and a song you hear though you shut your ears.

It is not the sap within the furrowed bark, nor a wing attached to a claw,

But rather a garden for ever in bloom and a flock of angels for ever in flight.

People of Orphalese, beauty is life when life unveils her holy face.

But you are life and you are the veil.

Beauty is eternity gazing at itself in a mirror.

But you are eternity and you are the mirror.

On Religion

And an old priest said, Speak to us of Religion.
And he said:
Have I spoken this day of aught else?
Is not religion all deeds and all reflection,
And that which is neither deed nor reflection, but a wonder and a surprise ever springing in the soul, even while the hands hew the stone or tend the loom?
Who can separate his faith from his actions, or his belief from his occupations?
Who can spread his hours before him, saying, "This for God and this for myself; This for my soul, and this other for my body?"
All your hours are wings that beat through space from self to self.
He who wears his morality but as his best garment were better naked.
The wind and the sun will tear no holes in his skin.
And he who defines his conduct by ethics imprisons his song-bird in a cage.
The freest song comes not through bars and wires.
And he to whom worshipping is a window, to open but also to shut, has not yet visited the house of his soul whose windows are from dawn to dawn.
Your daily life is your temple and your religion.
Whenever you enter into it take with you your all.
Take the plough and the forge and the mallet and the lute,

The things you have fashioned in necessity or for delight.

For in revery you cannot rise above your achievements nor fall lower than your failures.

And take with you all men:

For in adoration you cannot fly higher than their hopes nor humble yourself lower than their despair.

And if you would know God be not therefore a solver of riddles.

Rather look about you and you shall see Him playing with your children.

And look into space; you shall see Him walking in the cloud, outstretching His arms in the lightning and descending in rain.

You shall see Him smiling in flowers, then rising and waving His hands in trees.

On Death

Then Almitra spoke, saying, We would ask now of Death. And he said:

You would know the secret of death.

But how shall you find it unless you seek it in the heart of life?

The owl whose night-bound eyes are blind unto the day cannot unveil the mystery of light.

If you would indeed behold the spirit of death, open your heart wide unto the body of life.

For life and death are one, even as the river and the sea are one.

In the depth of your hopes and desires lies your silent knowledge of the beyond;

And like seeds dreaming beneath the snow your heart dreams of spring.

Trust the dreams, for in them is hidden the gate to eternity.

Your fear of death is but the trembling of the shepherd when he stands before the king whose hand is to be laid upon him in honour.

Is the shepherd not joyful beneath his trembling, that he shall wear the mark of the king?

Yet is he not more mindful of his trembling?

For what is it to die but to stand naked in the wind and to melt into the sun?

And what is it to cease breathing, but to free the

breath from its restless tides, that it may rise and expand and seek God unencumbered?

Only when you drink from the river of silence shall you indeed sing.

And when you have reached the mountain top, then you shall begin to climb.

And when the earth shall claim your limbs, then shall you truly dance.

The Farewell

And now it was evening.

And Almitra the seeress said, Blessed be this day and this place and your spirit that has spoken.

And he answered, Was it I who spoke? Was I not also a listener?

Then he descended the steps of the Temple and all the people followed him. And he reached his ship and stood upon the deck.

And facing the people again, he raised his voice and said:

People of Orphalese, the wind bids me leave you.

Less hasty am I than the wind, yet I must go.

We wanderers, ever seeking the lonelier way, begin no day where we have ended another day; and no sunrise finds us where sunset left us.

Even while the earth sleeps we travel.

We are the seeds of the tenacious plant, and it is in our ripeness and our fullness of heart that we are given to the wind and are scattered.

Brief were my days among you, and briefer still the words I have spoken.

But should my voice fade in your ears, and my love vanish in your memory, then I will come again,

And with a richer heart and lips more yielding to the spirit will I speak.

Yea, I shall return with the tide,

And though death may hide me, and the greater silence enfold me, yet again will I seek your understanding.

And not in vain will I seek.

If aught I have said is truth, that truth shall reveal itself in a clearer voice, and in words more kin to your thoughts.

I go with the wind, people of Orphalese, but not down into emptiness;

And if this day is not a fulfilment of your needs and my love, then let it be a promise till another day.

Man's needs change, but not his love, nor his desire that his love should satisfy his needs.

Know therefore, that from the greater silence I shall return.

The mist that drifts away at dawn, leaving but dew in the fields, shall rise and gather into a cloud and then fall down in rain.

And not unlike the mist have I been.

In the stillness of the night I have walked in your streets, and my spirit has entered your houses,

And your heart-beats were in my heart, and your breath was upon my face, and I knew you all.

Ay, I knew your joy and your pain, and in your sleep your dreams were my dreams.

And oftentimes I was among you a lake among the mountains.

I mirrored the summits in you and the bending slopes, and even the passing flocks of your thoughts and your desires.

And to my silence came the laughter of your children in streams, and the longing of your youths in rivers.

And when they reached my depth the streams and the rivers ceased not yet to sing.

But sweeter still than laughter and greater than longing came to me.

It was the boundless in you;

The vast man in whom you are all but cells and sinews;

He in whose chant all your singing is but a soundless throbbing.

It is in the vast man that you are vast,

And in beholding him that I beheld you and loved you.

For what distances can love reach that are not in that vast sphere?

What visions, what expectations and what presumptions can outsoar that flight?

Like a giant oak tree covered with apple blossoms is the vast man in you.

His might binds you to the earth, his fragrance lifts you into space, and in his durability you are deathless.

You have been told that, even like a chain, you are as weak as your weakest link.

This is but half the truth. You are also as strong as your strongest link.

To measure you by your smallest deed is to reckon the power of ocean by the frailty of its foam.

To judge you by your failures is to cast blame upon the seasons for their inconstancy.

Ay, you are like an ocean,

And though heavy-grounded ships await the tide upon your shores, yet, even like an ocean, you cannot hasten your tides.

And like the seasons you are also,

And though in your winter you deny your spring,

Yet spring, reposing within you, smiles in her drowsiness and is not offended.

Think not I say these things in order that you may say the one to the other, "He praised us well. He saw but the good in us."

I only speak to you in words of that which you yourselves know in thought.

And what is word knowledge but a shadow of wordless knowledge?

Your thoughts and my words are waves from a sealed memory that keeps records of our yesterdays,

And of the ancient days when the earth knew not us nor herself,

And of nights when earth was up-wrought with confusion.

Wise men have come to you to give you of their wisdom. I came to take of your wisdom:

And behold I have found that which is greater than wisdom.

It is a flame spirit in you ever gathering more of itself,

While you, heedless of its expansion, bewail the withering of your days.

It is life in quest of life in bodies that fear the grave.

There are no graves here.

These mountains and plains are a cradle and a stepping-stone.

Whenever you pass by the field where you have laid your ancestors look well thereupon, and you shall see yourselves and your children dancing hand in hand.

Verily you often make merry without knowing.

Others have come to you to whom for golden promises made unto your faith you have given but riches and power and glory.

Less than a promise have I given, and yet more generous have you been to me.

You have given me my deeper thirsting after life.

Surely there is no greater gift to a man than that which turns all his aims into parching lips and all life into a fountain.

And in this lies my honour and my reward,--

That whenever I come to the fountain to drink I find the living water itself thirsty;

And it drinks me while I drink it.

Some of you have deemed me proud and over-shy to receive gifts.

Too proud indeed am I to receive wages, but not gifts.

And though I have eaten berries among the hills when you would have had me sit at your board,

And slept in the portico of the temple when you would gladly have sheltered me,

Yet was it not your loving mindfulness of my days and my nights that made food sweet to my mouth and girdled my sleep with visions?

For this I bless you most:

You give much and know not that you give at all.

Verily the kindness that gazes upon itself in a mirror turns to stone,

And a good deed that calls itself by tender names becomes the parent to a curse.

And some of you have called me aloof, and drunk with my own aloneness,

And you have said, "He holds council with the trees of the forest, but not with men.

He sits alone on hill-tops and looks down upon our city."

True it is that I have climbed the hills and walked in remote places.

How could I have seen you save from a great height or a great distance?

How can one be indeed near unless he be far?

And others among you called unto me, not in words, and they said,

"Stranger, stranger, lover of unreachable heights, why dwell you among the summits where eagles build their nests?

Why seek you the unattainable?

What storms would you trap in your net,

And what vaporous birds do you hunt in the sky?

Come and be one of us.

Descend and appease your hunger with our bread and quench your thirst with our wine."

In the solitude of their souls they said these things;

But were their solitude deeper they would have known that I sought but the secret of your joy and your pain,

And I hunted only your larger selves that walk the sky.

But the hunter was also the hunted;

For many of my arrows left my bow only to seek my own breast.

And the flier was also the creeper;

For when my wings were spread in the sun their shadow upon the earth was a turtle.

And I the believer was also the doubter;

For often have I put my finger in my own wound that I might have the greater belief in you and the greater knowledge of you.

And it is with this belief and this knowledge that I say,

You are not enclosed within your bodies, nor confined to houses or fields.

That which is you dwells above the mountain and roves with the wind.

It is not a thing that crawls into the sun for warmth or digs holes into darkness for safety,

But a thing free, a spirit that envelops the earth and moves in the ether.

If these be vague words, then seek not to clear them.

Vague and nebulous is the beginning of all things, but not their end,

And I fain would have you remember me as a beginning.

Life, and all that lives, is conceived in the mist and not in the crystal.

And who knows but a crystal is mist in decay?

This would I have you remember in remembering me:

That which seems most feeble and bewildered in you is the strongest and most determined.

Is it not your breath that has erected and hardened the structure of your bones?

And is it not a dream which none of you remember having dreamt, that built your city and fashioned all there is in it?

Could you but see the tides of that breath you would cease to see all else,

And if you could hear the whispering of the dream you would hear no other sound.

But you do not see, nor do you hear, and it is well.

The veil that clouds your eyes shall be lifted by the hands that wove it,

And the clay that fills your ears shall be pierced by those fingers that kneaded it.

And you shall see.

And you shall hear.

Yet you shall not deplore having known blindness, nor regret having been deaf.

For in that day you shall know the hidden purposes in all things,

And you shall bless darkness as you would bless light.

After saying these things he looked about him, and he saw the pilot of his ship standing by the helm and gazing now at the full sails and now at the distance.

And he said:

Patient, over patient, is the captain of my ship.

The wind blows, and restless are the sails;

Even the rudder begs direction;

Yet quietly my captain awaits my silence.

And these my mariners, who have heard the choir of the greater sea, they too have heard me patiently.

Now they shall wait no longer.

I am ready.

The stream has reached the sea, and once more the great mother holds her son against her breast.

Fare you well, people of Orphalese.

This day has ended.

It is closing upon us even as the water-lily upon its own tomorrow.

What was given us here we shall keep,

And if it suffices not, then again must we come together and together stretch our hands unto the giver.

Forget not that I shall come back to you.

A little while, and my longing shall gather dust and foam for another body.

A little while, a moment of rest upon the wind, and another woman shall bear me.

Farewell to you and the youth I have spent with you.

It was but yesterday we met in a dream.

You have sung to me in my aloneness, and I of your longings have built a tower in the sky.

But now our sleep has fled and our dream is over, and it is no longer dawn.

The noontide is upon us and our half waking has turned to fuller day, and we must part.

If in the twilight of memory we should meet once more, we shall speak again together and you shall sing to me a deeper song.

And if our hands should meet in another dream we shall build another tower in the sky.

So saying he made a signal to the seamen, and straightway they weighed anchor and cast the ship loose from its moorings, and they moved eastward.

And a cry came from the people as from a single heart, and it rose into the dusk and was carried out over the sea like a great trumpeting.

Only Almitra was silent, gazing after the ship until it had vanished into the mist.

And when all the people were dispersed she still stood alone upon the sea-wall, remembering in her heart his saying,

"A little while, a moment of rest upon the wind, and another woman shall bear me."

THE MADMAN
HIS PARABLES AND POEMS

You ask me how I became a madman. It happened thus: One day, long before many gods were born, I woke from a deep sleep and found all my masks were stolen,--the seven masks I have fashioned and worn in seven lives,--I ran maskless through the crowded streets shouting, "Thieves, thieves, the cursed thieves."

Men and women laughed at me and some ran to their houses in fear of me.

And when I reached the market place, a youth standing on a house-top cried, "He is a madman." I looked up to behold him; the sun kissed my own naked face for the first time. For the first time the sun kissed my own naked face and my soul was inflamed with love for the sun, and I wanted my masks no more. And as if in a trance I cried, "Blessed, blessed are the thieves who stole my masks."

Thus I became a madman.

And I have found both freedom and safety in my madness; the freedom of loneliness and the safety from being understood, for those who understand us enslave something in us.

But let me not be too proud of my safety. Even a Thief in a jail is safe from another thief.

God

In the ancient days, when the first quiver of speech came to my lips, I ascended the holy mountain and spoke unto God, saying, "Master, I am thy slave. Thy hidden will is my law and I shall obey thee for ever more."

But God made no answer, and like a mighty tempest passed away.

And after a thousand years I ascended the holy mountain and again spoke unto God, saying, "Creator, I am thy creation. Out of clay hast thou fashioned me and to thee I owe mine all."

And God made no answer, but like a thousand swift wings passed away.

And after a thousand years I climbed the holy mountain and spoke unto God again, saying, "Father, I am thy son. In pity and love thou hast given me birth, and through love and worship I shall inherit thy kingdom."

And God made no answer, and like the mist that veils the distant hills he passed away.

And after a thousand years I climbed the sacred mountain and again spoke unto God, saying, "My God, my aim and my fulfillment; I am thy yesterday and thou are my tomorrow. I am thy root in the earth and thou art my flower in the sky, and together we grow before the face of the sun."

Then God leaned over me, and in my ears whispered words of sweetness, and even as the sea that enfoldeth a brook that runneth down to her, he enfolded me.

And when I descended to the valleys and the plains God was there also.

My Friend

My friend, I am not what I seem. Seeming is but a garment I wear--a care-woven garment that protects me from thy questionings and thee from my negligence.

The "I" in me, my friend, dwells in the house of silence, and therein it shall remain for ever more, unperceived, unapproachable.

I would not have thee believe in what I say nor trust in what I do--for my words are naught but thy own thoughts in sound and my deeds thy own hopes in action.

When thou sayest, "The wind bloweth eastward," I say, "Aye it doth blow eastward"; for I would not have thee know that my mind doth not dwell upon the wind but upon the sea.

Thou canst not understand my seafaring thoughts, nor would I have thee understand. I would be at sea alone.

When it is day with thee, my friend, it is night with me; yet even then I speak of the noontide that dances upon the hills and of the purple shadow that steals its way across the valley; for thou canst not hear the songs of my darkness nor see my wings beating against the stars--and I fain would not have thee hear or see. I would be with night alone.

When thou ascendest to thy Heaven I descend to my Hell--even then thou callest to me across the unbridgeable gulf, "My companion, my comrade," and I call back to thee, "My comrade, my companion"--for I would not have thee see my Hell. The flame would burn thy eyesight and the smoke would crowd thy nostrils. And I love my Hell too well to have thee visit it. I would be in Hell alone.

Thou lovest Truth and Beauty and Righteousness; and I for thy sake say it is well and seemly to love these things. But in my heart I laugh at thy love. Yet I would not have thee see my laughter. I would laugh alone.

My friend, thou art good and cautious and wise; nay, thou art perfect--and I, too, speak with thee wisely and cautiously. And yet I am mad. But I mask my madness. I would be mad alone.

My friend, thou art not my friend, but how shall I make thee understand? My path is not thy path, yet together we walk, hand in hand.

The Scarecrow

Once I said to a scarecrow, "You must be tired of standing in this lonely field."

And he said, "The joy of scaring is a deep and lasting one, and I never tire of it."

Said I, after a minute of thought, "It is true; for I too have known that joy."

Said he, "Only those who are stuffed with straw can know it."

Then I left him, not knowing whether he had complimented or belittled me.

A year passed, during which the scarecrow turned philosopher.

And when I passed by him again I saw two crows building a nest under his hat.

The Sleep-Walkers

In the town where I was born lived a woman and her daughter, who walked in their sleep.

One night, while silence enfolded the world, the woman and her daughter, walking, yet asleep, met in their mist-veiled garden.

And the mother spoke, and she said: "At last, at last, my enemy! You by whom my youth was destroyed--who have built up your life upon the ruins of mine! Would I could kill you!"

And the daughter spoke, and she said: "O hateful woman, selfish and old! Who stand between my freer self and me! Who would have my life an echo of your own faded life! Would you were dead!"

At that moment a cock crew, and both women awoke. The mother said gently, "Is that you, darling?" And the daughter answered gently, "Yes, dear."

The Wise Dog

One day there passed by a company of cats a wise dog. And as he came near and saw that they were very intent and heeded him not, he stopped.

Then there arose in the midst of the company a large, grave cat and looked upon them and said, "Brethren, pray ye; and when ye have prayed again and yet again, nothing doubting, verily then it shall rain mice."

And when the dog heard this he laughed in his heart and turned from them saying, "O blind and foolish cats, has it not been written and have I not known and my fathers before me, that that which raineth for prayer and faith and supplication is not mice but bones."

The Two Hermits

Upon a lonely mountain, there lived two hermits who worshipped God and loved one another.

Now these two hermits had one earthen bowl, and this was their only possession.

One day an evil spirit entered into the heart of the older hermit and he came to the younger and said, "It is long that we have lived together. The time has come for us to part. Let us divide our possessions."

Then the younger hermit was saddened and he said, "It grieves me, Brother, that thou shouldst leave me. But if thou must needs go, so be it," and he brought the earthen bowl and gave it to him saying, "We cannot divide it, Brother, let it be thine."

Then the older hermit said, "Charity I will not accept. I will take nothing but mine own. It must be divided."

And the younger one said, "If the bowl be broken, of what use would it be to thee or to me? If it be thy pleasure let us rather cast a lot."

But the older hermit said again, "I will have but justice and mine own, and I will not trust justice and mine own to vain chance. The bowl must be divided."

Then the younger hermit could reason no further and he said, "If it be indeed thy will, and if even so thou wouldst have it let us now break the bowl."

But the face of the older hermit grew exceedingly dark, and he cried, "O thou cursed coward, thou wouldst not fight."

On Giving and Taking

Once there lived a man who had a valley-full of needles. And one day the mother of Jesus came to him and said: "Friend, my son's garment is torn and I must needs mend it before he goeth to the temple. Wouldst thou not give me a needle?"

And he gave her not a needle, but he gave her a learned discourse on Giving and Taking to carry to her son before he should go to the temple.

The Seven Selves

In the stillest hour of the night, as I lay half asleep, my seven selves sat together and thus conversed in whisper:

First Self: Here, in this madman, I have dwelt all these years, with naught to do but renew his pain by day and recreate his sorrow by night. I can bear my fate no longer, and now I rebel.

Second Self: Yours is a better lot than mine, brother, for it is given to me to be this madman's joyous self. I laugh his laughter and sing his happy hours, and with thrice winged feet I dance his brighter thoughts. It is I that would rebel against my weary existence.

Third Self: And what of me, the love-ridden self, the flaming brand of wild passion and fantastic desires? It is I the love-sick self who would rebel against this madman.

Fourth Self: I, amongst you all, am the most miserable, for naught was given me but odious hatred and destructive loathing. It is I, the tempest-like self, the one born in the black caves of Hell, who would protest against serving this madman.

Fifth Self: Nay, it is I, the thinking self, the fanciful self, the self of hunger and thirst, the one doomed to wander without rest in search of unknown things and things not yet created; it is I, not you, who would rebel.

Sixth Self: And I, the working self, the pitiful labourer, who, with patient hands, and longing eyes, fashion the days into images and give the formless elements new and eternal forms--it is I, the solitary one, who would rebel against this restless madman.

Seventh Self: How strange that you all would rebel against this man, because each and every one of you has a preordained fate to fulfill. Ah! could I but be like one of you, a self with a determined lot! But I have none, I am the do-nothing self, the one who sits in the dumb, empty nowhere and nowhen, while you are busy re-creating life. Is it you or I, neighbours, who should rebel?

When the seventh self thus spake the other six selves looked with pity upon him but said nothing more; and as the night grew deeper one after the other went to sleep enfolded with a new and happy submission.

But the seventh self remained watching and gazing at nothingness, which is behind all things.

War

One night a feast was held in the palace, and there came a man and prostrated himself before the prince, and all the feasters looked upon him; and they saw that one of his eyes was out and that the empty socket bled. And the prince inquired of him, "What has befallen you?" And the man replied, "O prince, I am by profession a thief, and this night, because there was no moon, I went to rob the money-changer's shop, and as I climbed in through the window I made a mistake and entered the weaver's shop, and in the dark I ran into the weaver's loom and my eye was plucked out. And now, O prince, I ask for justice upon the weaver."

Then the prince sent for the weaver and he came, and it was decreed that one of his eyes should be plucked out.

"O prince," said the weaver, "the decree is just. It is right that one of my eyes be taken. And yet, alas! both are necessary to me in order that I may see the two sides of the cloth that I weave. But I have a neighbour, a cobbler, who has also two eyes, and in his trade both eyes are not necessary."

Then the prince sent for the cobbler. And he came. And they took out one of the cobbler's two eyes.

And justice was satisfied.

The Fox

A fox looked at his shadow at sunrise and said, "I will have a camel for lunch today." And all morning he went about looking for camels. But at noon he saw his shadow again--and he said, "A mouse will do."

The Wise King

Once there ruled in the distant city of Wirani a king who was both mighty and wise. And he was feared for his might and loved for his wisdom.

Now, in the heart of that city was a well, whose water was cool and crystalline, from which all the inhabitants drank, even the king and his courtiers; for there was no other well.

One night when all were asleep, a witch entered the city, and poured seven drops of strange liquid into the well, and said, "From this hour he who drinks this water shall become mad."

Next morning all the inhabitants, save the king and his lord chamberlain, drank from the well and became mad, even as the witch had foretold.

And during that day the people in the narrow streets and in the market places did naught but whisper to one another, "The king is mad. Our king and his lord chamberlain have lost their reason. Surely we cannot be ruled by a mad king. We must dethrone him."

That evening the king ordered a golden goblet to be filled from the well. And when it was brought to him he drank deeply, and gave it to his lord chamberlain to drink.

And there was great rejoicing in that distant city of Wirani, because its king and its lord chamberlain had regained their reason.

Ambition

Three men met at a tavern table. One was a weaver, another a carpenter and the third a ploughman.

Said the weaver, "I sold a fine linen shroud today for two pieces of gold. Let us have all the wine we want."

"And I," said the carpenter, "I sold my best coffin. We will have a great roast with the wine."

"I only dug a grave," said the ploughman, "but my patron paid me double. Let us have honey cakes too."

And all that evening the tavern was busy, for they called often for wine and meat and cakes. And they were merry.

And the host rubbed his hands and smiled at his wife; for his guests were spending freely.

When they left the moon was high, and they walked along the road singing and shouting together.

The host and his wife stood in the tavern door and looked after them.

"Ah!" said the wife, "these gentlemen! So freehanded and so gay! If only they could bring us such luck every day! Then our son need not be a tavern-keeper and work so hard. We could educate him, and he could become a priest."

The New Pleasure

Last night I invented a new pleasure, and as I was giving it the first trial an angel and a devil came rushing toward my house. They met at my door and fought with each other over my newly created pleasure; the one crying, "It is a sin!"--the other, "It is a virtue!"

The Other Language

Three days after I was born, as I lay in my silken cradle, gazing with astonished dismay on the new world round about me, my mother spoke to the wet-nurse, saying, "How does my child?"

And the wet-nurse answered, "He does well, Madame, I have fed him three times; and never before have I seen a babe so young yet so gay."

And I was indignant; and I cried, "It is not true, mother; for my bed is hard, and the milk I have sucked is bitter to my mouth, and the odour of the breast is foul in my nostrils, and I am most miserable."

But my mother did not understand, nor did the nurse; for the language I spoke was that of the world from which I came.

And on the twenty-first day of my life, as I was being christened, the priest said to my mother, "You should indeed by happy, Madame, that your son was born a Christian."

And I was surprised,--and I said to the priest, "Then your mother in Heaven should be unhappy, for you were not born a Christian."

But the priest too did not understand my language.

And after seven moons, one day a soothsayer looked at me, and he said to my mother, "Your son will be a statesman and a great leader of men."

But I cried out,--"That is a false prophet; for I shall be a musician, and naught but a musician shall I be."

But even at that age my language was not understood--and great was my astonishment.

And after three and thirty years, during which my mother, and the nurse, and the priest have all died, (the shadow of God be upon their spirits) the soothsayer still lives. And yesterday I met him near the gates of the temple; and while we were talking together he said, "I have always known you would become a great musician. Even in your infancy I prophesied and foretold your future."

And I believed him--for now I too have forgotten the language of that other world.

The Pomegranate

Once when I was living in the heart of a pomegranate, I heard a seed saying, "Someday I shall become a tree, and the wind will sing in my branches, and the sun will dance on my leaves, and I shall be strong and beautiful through all the seasons."

Then another seed spoke and said, "When I was as young as you, I too held such views; but now that I can weigh and measure things, I see that my hopes were vain."

And a third seed spoke also, "I see in us nothing that promises so great a future."

And a fourth said, "But what a mockery our life would be, without a greater future!"

Said a fifth, "Why dispute what we shall be, when we know not even what we are."

But a sixth replied, "Whatever we are, that we shall continue to be."

And a seventh said, "I have such a clear idea how everything will be, but I cannot put it into words."

Then an eight spoke--and a ninth--and a tenth--and then many--until all were speaking, and I could distinguish nothing for the many voices.

And so I moved that very day into the heart of a quince, where the seeds are few and almost silent.

The Two Cages

In my father's garden there are two cages. In one is a lion, which my father's slaves brought from the desert of Ninavah; in the other is a songless sparrow.

Every day at dawn the sparrow calls to the lion, "Good morrow to thee, brother prisoner."

The Three Ants

Three ants met on the nose of a man who was asleep in the sun. And after they had saluted one another, each according to the custom of his tribe, they stood there conversing.

The first ant said, "These hills and plains are the most barren I have known. I have searched all day for a grain of some sort, and there is none to be found."

Said the second ant, "I too have found nothing, though I have visited every nook and glade. This is, I believe, what my people call the soft, moving land where nothing grows."

Then the third ant raised his head and said, "My friends, we are standing now on the nose of the Supreme Ant, the mighty and infinite Ant, whose body is so great that we cannot see it, whose shadow is so vast that we cannot trace it, whose voice is so loud that we cannot hear it; and He is omnipresent."

When the third ant spoke thus the other ants looked at each other and laughed.

At that moment the man moved and in his sleep raised his hand and scratched his nose, and the three ants were crushed.

The Grave-Digger

Once, as I was burying one of my dead selves, the grave-digger came by and said to me, "Of all those who come here to bury, you alone I like."

Said I, "You please me exceedingly, but why do you like me?"

"Because," said he, "They come weeping and go weeping--you only come laughing and go laughing."

On the Steps of the Temple

Yestereve, on the marble steps of the Temple, I saw a woman sitting between two men. One side of her face was pale, the other was blushing.

The Blessed City

In my youth I was told that in a certain city every one lived according to the Scriptures.

And I said, "I will seek that city and the blessedness thereof." And it was far. And I made great provision for my journey. And after forty days I beheld the city and on the forty-first day I entered into it.

And lo! the whole company of the inhabitants had each but a single eye and but one hand. And I was astonished and said to myself, "Shall they of this so holy city have but one eye and one hand?"

Then I saw that they too were astonished, for they were marveling greatly at my two hands and my two eyes. And as they were speaking together I inquired of them saying, "Is this indeed the Blessed City, where each man lives according to the Scriptures?" And they said, "Yes, this is that city."

"And what," said I, "hath befallen you, and where are your right eyes and your right hands?"

And all the people were moved. And they said, "Come thou and see."

And they took me to the temple in the midst of the city. And in the temple I saw a heap of hands and eyes. All withered. Then said I, "Alas! what conqueror hath committed this cruelty upon you?"

And there went a murmur amongst them. And one of their elders stood forth and said, "This doing is of ourselves. God hath made us conquerors over the evil that was in us."

And he led me to a high altar, and all the people followed. And he showed me above the altar an inscription graven, and I read:

"If thy right eye offend thee, pluck it out and cast it from thee; for it is profitable for thee that one of thy members should perish, and not that the whole body should be cast into hell. And if thy right hand offend thee, cut it off and cast it from thee; for it is profitable for thee that one of thy members should perish, and not that thy whole body should be cast into hell."

Then I understood. And I turned about to all the people and cried, "Hath no man or woman among you two eyes or two hands?"

And they answered me saying, "No, not one. There is none whole save such as are yet too young to read the Scripture and to understand its commandment."

And when we had come out of the temple, I straightway left that Blessed City; for I was not too young, and I could read the scripture.

The Good God and the Evil God

The Good God and the Evil God met on the mountain top.

The Good God said, "Good day to you, brother."

The Evil God did not answer.

And the Good God said, "You are in a bad humour today."

"Yes," said the Evil God, "for of late I have been often mistaken for you, called by your name, and treated as if I were you, and it ill-pleases me."

And the Good God said, "But I too have been mistaken for you and called by your name."

The Evil God walked away cursing the stupidity of man.

Defeat

Defeat, my Defeat, my solitude and my aloofness; You are dearer to me than a thousand triumphs, And sweeter to my heart than all world-glory.

Defeat, my Defeat, my self-knowledge and my defiance, Through you I know that I am yet young and swift of foot And not to be trapped by withering laurels. And in you I have found aloneness And the joy of being shunned and scorned.

Defeat, my Defeat, my shining sword and shield, In your eyes I have read That to be enthroned is to be enslaved, And to be understood is to be leveled down, And to be grasped is but to reach one's fullness And like a ripe fruit to fall and be consumed.

Defeat, my Defeat, my bold companion, You shall hear my songs and my cries and my silences, And none but you shall speak to me of the beating of wings, And urging of seas, And of mountains that burn in the night, And you alone shall climb my steep and rocky soul.

Defeat, my Defeat, my deathless courage, You and I shall laugh together with the storm, And together we shall dig graves for all that die in us, And we shall stand in the sun with a will, And we shall be dangerous.

Night and the Madman

"I am like thee, O, Night, dark and naked; I walk on the flaming path which is above my day-dreams, and whenever my foot touches earth a giant oak tree comes forth."

"Nay, thou art not like me, O, Madman, for thou still lookest backward to see how large a foot-print thou leavest on the sand."

"I am like thee, O, Night, silent and deep; and in the heart of my loneliness lies a Goddess in child-bed; and in him who is being born Heaven touches Hell."

"Nay, thou art not like me, O, Madman, for thou shudderest yet before pain, and the song of the abyss terrifies thee."

"I am like thee, O, Night, wild and terrible; for my ears are crowded with cries of conquered nations and sighs for forgotten lands."

"Nay, thou art not like me, O, Madman, for thou still takest thy little-self for a comrade, and with thy monster-self thou canst not be friend."

"I am like thee, O, Night, cruel and awful; for my bosom is lit by burning ships at sea, and my lips are wet with blood of slain warriors."

"Nay, thou art not like me, O, Madman; for the desire for a sister-spirit is yet upon thee, and thou has not become alone unto thyself."

"I am like thee, O, Night, joyous and glad; for he who

dwells in my shadow is now drunk with virgin wine, and she who follows me is sinning mirthfully."

"Nay, thou art not like me, O, Madman, for thy soul is wrapped in the veil of seven folds and thou holdest not thy heart in thine hand."

"I am like thee, O, Night, patient and passionate; for in my breast a thousand dead lovers are buried in shrouds of withered kisses."

"Yea, Madman, art thou like me? Art thou like me? And canst thou ride the tempest as a steed, and grasp the lightning as a sword?"

"Like thee, O, Night, like thee, mighty and high, and my throne is built upon heaps of fallen Gods; and before me too pass the days to kiss the hem of my garment but never to gaze at my face."

"Art thou like me, child of my darkest heart? And dost thou think my untamed thoughts and speak my vast language?"

"Yea, we are twin brothers, O, Night; for thou revealest space and I reveal my soul."

Faces

I have seen a face with a thousand countenances, and a face that was but a single countenance as if held in a mould.

I have seen a face whose sheen I could look through to the ugliness beneath, and a face whose sheen I had to lift to see how beautiful it was.

I have seen an old face much lined with nothing, and a smooth face in which all things were graven.

I know faces, because I look through the fabric my own eye weaves, and behold the reality beneath.

The Greater Sea

My soul and I went to the great sea to bathe. And when we reached the shore, we went about looking for a hidden and lonely place.

But as we walked, we saw a man sitting on a grey rock taking pinches of salt from a bag and throwing them into the sea.

"This is the pessimist," said my soul, "Let us leave this place. We cannot bathe here."

We walked on until we reached an inlet. There we saw, standing on a white rock, a man holding a bejeweled box, from which he took sugar and threw it into the sea.

"And this is the optimist," said my soul, "And he too must not see our naked bodies."

Further on we walked. And on a beach we saw a man picking up dead fish and tenderly putting them back into the water.

"And we cannot bathe before him," said my soul. "He is the humane philanthropist."

And we passed on.

Then we came where we saw a man tracing his shadow on the sand. Great waves came and erased it. But he went on tracing it again and again.

"He is the mystic," said my soul, "Let us leave him."

And we walked on, till in a quiet cover we saw a man scooping up the foam and putting it into an alabaster bowl.

"He is the idealist," said my soul, "Surely he must not see our nudity."

And on we walked. Suddenly we heard a voice crying, "This is the sea. This is the deep sea. This is the vast and mighty sea." And when we reached the voice it was a man whose back was turned to the sea, and at his ear he held a shell, listening to its murmur.

And my soul said, "Let us pass on. He is the realist, who turns his back on the whole he cannot grasp, and busies himself with a fragment."

So we passed on. And in a weedy place among the rocks was a man with his head buried in the sand. And I said to my soul, "We can bath here, for he cannot see us."

"Nay," said my soul, "For he is the most deadly of them all. He is the puritan."

Then a great sadness came over the face of my soul, and into her voice.

"Let us go hence," she said, "For there is no lonely, hidden place where we can bathe. I would not have this wind lift my golden hair, or bare my white bosom in this air, or let the light disclose my sacred nakedness."

Then we left that sea to seek the Greater Sea.

Crucified

I cried to men, "I would be crucified!"
And they said, "Why should your blood be upon our heads?"

And I answered, "How else shall you be exalted except by crucifying madmen?"

And they heeded and I was crucified. And the crucifixion appeased me.

And when I was hanged between earth and heaven they lifted up their heads to see me. And they were exalted, for their heads had never before been lifted.

But as they stood looking up at me one called out, "For what art thou seeking to atone?"

And another cried, "In what cause dost thou sacrifice thyself?"

And a third said, "Thinkest thou with this price to buy world glory?"

Then said a fourth, "Behold, how he smiles! Can such pain be forgiven?"

And I answered them all, and said:

"Remember only that I smiled. I do not atone--nor sacrifice--nor wish for glory; and I have nothing to forgive. I thirsted--and I besought you to give me my blood to drink. For what is there can quench a madman's thirst but his own blood? I was dumb--and I asked wounds of you for mouths. I was imprisoned in your days and nights--and I sought a door into larger days and nights.

And now I go--as others already crucified have gone. And think not we are weary of crucifixion. For we must be crucified by larger and yet larger men, between greater earths and greater heavens."

The Astronomer

In the shadow of the temple my friend and I saw a blind man sitting alone. And my friend said, "Behold the wisest man of our land."

Then I left my friend and approached the blind man and greeted him. And we conversed.

After a while I said, "Forgive my question; but since when has thou been blind?"

"From my birth," he answered.

Said I, "And what path of wisdom followest thou?"

Said he, "I am an astronomer."

Then he placed his hand upon his breast saying, "I watch all these suns and moons and stars."

The Great Longing

Here I sit between my brother the mountain and my sister the sea.

We three are one in loneliness, and the love that binds us together is deep and strong and strange. Nay, it is deeper than my sister's depth and stronger than my brother's strength, and stranger than the strangeness of my madness.

Aeons upon aeons have passed since the first grey dawn made us visible to one another; and though we have seen the birth and the fullness and the death of many worlds, we are still eager and young.

We are young and eager and yet we are mateless and unvisited, and though we lie in unbroken half embrace, we are uncomforted. And what comfort is there for controlled desire and unspent passion? Whence shall come the flaming god to warm my sister's bed? And what she-torrent shall quench my brother's fire? And who is the woman that shall command my heart?

In the stillness of the night my sister murmurs in her sleep the fire-god's unknown name, and my brother calls afar upon the cool and distant goddess. But upon whom I call in my sleep I know not.

*

Here I sit between my brother the mountain and my sister the sea. We three are one in loneliness, and the love that binds us together is deep and strong and strange.

Said a Blade of Grass

Said a blade of grass to an autumn leaf, "You make such a noise falling! You scatter all my winter dreams."

Said the leaf indignant, "Low-born and low-dwelling! Songless, peevish thing! You live not in the upper air and you cannot tell the sound of singing."

Then the autumn leaf lay down upon the earth and slept. And when spring came she waked again--and she was a blade of grass.

And when it was autumn and her winter sleep was upon her, and above her through all the air the leaves were falling, she muttered to herself, "O these autumn leaves! They make such noise! They scatter all my winter dreams."

The Eye

Said the Eye one day, "I see beyond these valleys a mountain veiled with blue mist. Is it not beautiful?"

The Ear listened, and after listening intently awhile, said, "But where is any mountain? I do not hear it."

Then the Hand spoke and said, "I am trying in vain to feel it or touch it, and I can find no mountain."

And the Nose said, "There is no mountain, I cannot smell it."

Then the Eye turned the other way, and they all began to talk together about the Eye's strange delusion. And they said, "Something must be the matter with the Eye."

The Two Learned Men

Once there lived in the ancient city of Afkar two learned men who hated and belittled each other's learning. For one of them denied the existence of the gods and the other was a believer.

One day the two met in the marketplace, and amidst their followers they began to dispute and to argue about the existence or the non-existence of the gods. And after hours of contention they parted.

That evening the unbeliever went to the temple and prostrated himself before the altar and prayed the gods to forgive his wayward past.

And the same hour the other learned man, he who had upheld the gods, burned his sacred books. For he had become an unbeliever.

When My Sorrow Was Born

When my Sorrow was born I nursed it with care, and watched over it with loving tenderness.

And my Sorrow grew like all living things, strong and beautiful and full of wondrous delights.

And we loved one another, my Sorrow and I, and we loved the world about us; for Sorrow had a kindly heart and mine was kindly with Sorrow.

And when we conversed, my Sorrow and I, our days were winged and our nights were girdled with dreams; for Sorrow had an eloquent tongue, and mine was eloquent with Sorrow.

And when we sang together, my Sorrow and I, our neighbors sat at their windows and listened; for our songs were deep as the sea and our melodies were full of strange memories.

And when we walked together, my Sorrow and I, people gazed at us with gentle eyes and whispered in words of exceeding sweetness. And there were those who looked with envy upon us, for Sorrow was a noble thing and I was proud with Sorrow.

But my Sorrow died, like all living things, and alone I am left to muse and ponder.

And now when I speak my words fall heavily upon my ears.

And when I sing my songs my neighbours come not to listen.

And when I walk the streets no one looks at me.

Only in my sleep I hear voices saying in pity, "See, there lies the man whose Sorrow is dead."

And When my Joy was Born

And when my Joy was born, I held it in my arms and stood on the house-top shouting, "Come ye, my neighbours, come and see, for Joy this day is born unto me. Come and behold this gladsome thing that laugheth in the sun."

But none of my neighbours came to look upon my Joy, and great was my astonishment.

And every day for seven moons I proclaimed my Joy from the house-top--and yet no one heeded me. And my Joy and I were alone, unsought and unvisited.

Then my Joy grew pale and weary because no other heart but mine held its loveliness and no other lips kissed its lips.

Then my Joy died of isolation.

And now I only remember my dead Joy in remembering my dead Sorrow. But memory is an autumn leaf that murmurs a while in the wind and then is heard no more.

The Perfect World

God of lost souls, thou who are lost amongst the gods, hear me:

Gentle Destiny that watchest over us, mad, wandering spirits, hear me:

I dwell in the midst of a perfect race, I the most imperfect.

I, a human chaos, a nebula of confused elements, I move amongst finished worlds--peoples of complete laws and pure order, whose thoughts are assorted, whose dreams are arranged, and whose visions are enrolled and registered.

Their virtues, O God, are measured, their sins are weighed, and even the countless things that pass in the dim twilight of neither sin nor virtue are recorded and catalogued.

Here days and night are divided into seasons of conduct and governed by rules of blameless accuracy.

To eat, to drink, to sleep, to cover one's nudity, and then to be weary in due time.

To work, to play, to sing, to dance, and then to lie still when the clock strikes the hour.

To think thus, to feel thus much, and then to cease thinking and feeling when a certain star rises above yonder horizon.

To rob a neighbour with a smile, to bestow gifts with a graceful wave of the hand, to praise prudently, to blame cautiously, to destroy a sound with a word, to burn a body with a breath, and then to wash the hands when the day's work is done.

To love according to an established order, to entertain one's best self in a preconceived manner, to worship the gods becomingly, to intrigue the devils artfully--and then to forget all as though memory were dead.

To fancy with a motive, to contemplate with consideration, to be happy sweetly, to suffer nobly--and then to empty the cup so that tomorrow may fill it again.

All these things, O God, are conceived with forethought, born with determination, nursed with exactness, governed by rules, directed by reason, and then slain and buried after a prescribed method. And even their silent graves that lie within the human soul are marked and numbered.

It is a perfect world, a world of consummate excellence, a world of supreme wonders, the ripest fruit in God's garden, the master-thought of the universe.

But why should I be here, O God, I a green seed of unfulfilled passion, a mad tempest that seeketh neither east nor west, a bewildered fragment from a burnt planet?

Why am I here, O God of lost souls, thou who art lost amongst the gods?

THE FORERUNNER
HIS PARABLES AND POEMS

You are your own forerunner, and the towers you have builded are but the foundation of your giant-self. And that self too shall be a foundation.

And I too am my own forerunner, for the long shadow stretching before me at sunrise shall gather under my feet at the noon hour. Yet another sunrise shall lay another shadow before me, and that also shall be gathered at another noon.

Always have we been our own forerunners, and always shall we be. And all that we have gathered and shall gather shall be but seeds for fields yet unploughed. We are the fields and the ploughmen, the gatherers and the gathered.

When you were a wandering desire in the mist, I too was there, a wandering desire. Then we sought one another, and out of our eagerness dreams were born. And dreams were time limitless, and dreams were space without measure.

And when you were a silent word upon Life's quivering lips, I too was there, another silent word. Then Life uttered us and we came down the years throbbing with memories of yesterday and with longing for tomorrow, for yesterday was death conquered and tomorrow was birth pursued.

And now we are in God's hands. You are a sun in His right hand and I an earth in His left hand. Yet you are not more, shining, than I, shone upon.

And we, sun and earth, are but the beginning of a

greater sun and a greater earth. And always shall we be the beginning.

*

You are your own forerunner, you the stranger passing by the gate of my garden.

And I too am my own forerunner, though I sit in the shadows of my trees and seem motionless.

GOD'S FOOL

Once there came from the desert to the great city of Sharia a man who was a dreamer, and he had naught but his garment and a staff.

And as he walked through the streets he gazed with awe and wonder at the temples and towers and palaces, for the city of Sharia was of surpassing beauty. And he spoke often to the passersby, questioning them about their city--but they understood not his language, nor he their language.

At the noon hour he stopped before a vast inn. It was built of yellow marble, and people were going in and coming out unhindered.

"This must be a shrine," he said to himself, and he too went in. But what was his surprise to find himself in a hall of great splendour and a large company of men and women seated about many tables. They were eating and drinking and listening to the musicians.

"Nay," said the dreamer. "This is no worshipping. It must be a feast given by the prince to the people, in celebration of a great event."

At that moment a man, whom he took to be the slave of the prince, approached him, and bade him be seated. And he was served with meat and wine and most excellent sweets.

When he was satisfied, the dreamer rose to depart. At the door he was stopped by a large man magnificently arrayed.

"Surely this is the prince himself," said the dreamer in his heart, and he bowed to him and thanked him.

Then the large man said in the language of the city:

"Sir, you have not paid for your dinner." And the dreamer did not understand, and again thanked him heartily. Then the large man bethought him, and he looked more closely upon the dreamer. And he saw that he was a stranger, clad in but a poor garment, and that indeed he had not wherewith to pay for his meal. Then the large man clapped his hands and called--and there came four watchmen of the city. And they listened to the large man. Then they took the dreamer between them, and they were two on each side of him. And the dreamer noted the ceremoniousness of their dress and of their manner and he looked upon them with delight.

"These," said he, "are men of distinction."

And they walked all together until they came to the House of Judgment and they entered.

The dreamer saw before him, seated upon a throne, a venerable man with flowing beard, robed majestically. And he thought he was the king. And he rejoiced to be brought before him.

Now the watchmen related to the judge, who was the venerable man, the charge against the dreamer; and the judge appointed two advocates, one to present the charge and the other to defend the stranger. And the advocates rose, the one after the other, and delivered each his argument. And the dreamer thought himself to be listening to addresses of welcome, and his heart filled with gratitude to the king and the prince for all that was done for him.

Then sentence was passed upon the dreamer, that upon a tablet hung about his neck his crime should be written, and that he should ride through the city on a naked horse, with a trumpeter and a drummer before him. And the sentence was carried out forthwith.

Now as the dreamer rode through the city upon the naked horse, with the trumpeter and the drummer before him, the inhabitants of the city came running forth at the sound of the noise, and when they saw him they laughed one and all, and the children ran after him in companies from street to street. And the dreamer's heart was filled with ecstasy, and his eyes shone upon them. For to him the tablet was a sign of the king's blessing and the procession was in his honour.

Now as he rode, he saw among the crowd a man who was from the desert like himself and his heart swelled with joy, and he cried out to him with a shout:

"Friend! Friend! Where are we? What city of the heart's desire is this? What race of lavish hosts?--who feast the chance guest in their palaces, whose princes companion him, whose king hangs a token upon his breast and opens to him the hospitality of a city descended from heaven."

And he who was also of the desert replied not. He only smiled and slightly shook his head. And the procession passed on.

And the dreamer's face was uplifted and his eyes were overflowing with light.

LOVE

They say the jackal and the mole
Drink from the self-same stream
Where the lion comes to drink.

And they say the eagle and the vulture
Dig their beaks into the same carcass,
And are at peace, one with the other,
In the presence of the dead thing.
O love, whose lordly hand
Has bridled my desires,
And raised my hunger and my thirst
To dignity and pride,
Let not the strong in me and the constant
Eat the bread or drink the wine
That tempt my weaker self.
Let me rather starve,
And let my heart parch with thirst,
And let me die and perish,
Ere I stretch my hand
To a cup you did not fill,
Or a bowl you did not bless.

THE KING-HERMIT

They told me that in a forest among the mountains lives a young man in solitude who once was a king of a vast country beyond the Two Rivers. And they also said that he, of his own will, had left his throne and the land of his glory and come to dwell in the wilderness.

And I said, "I would seek that man, and learn the secret of his heart; for he who renounces a kingdom must needs be greater than a kingdom."

On that very day I went to the forest where he dwells. And I found him sitting under a white cypress, and in his hand a reed as if it were a sceptre. And I greeted him even as I would greet a king.

And he turned to me and said gently, "What would you in this forest of serenity? Seek you a lost self in the green shadows, or is it a home-coming in your twilight?"

And I answered, "I sought but you--for I fain would know that which made you leave a kingdom for a forest."

And he said, "Brief is my story, for sudden was the bursting of the bubble. It happened thus: One day as I sat at a window in my palace, my chamberlain and an envoy from a foreign land were walking in my garden. And as they approached my window, the lord chamberlain was speaking of himself and saying, 'I am like the king; I have a thirst for strong wine and a hunger for all games of chance. And like my lord the king I have storms of temper.' And the lord chamberlain and the envoy disappeared among the trees. But in a few minutes they returned, and this time the

lord chamberlain was speaking of me, and he was saying, 'My lord the king is like myself--a good marksman; and like me he loves music and bathes thrice a day.'"

After a moment he added, "On the eve of that day I left my palace with but my garment, for I would no longer be ruler over those who assume my vices and attribute to me their virtues."

And I said, "This is indeed a wonder, and passing strange."

And he said, "Nay, my friend, you knocked at the gate of my silences and received but a trifle. For who would not leave a kingdom for a forest where the seasons sing and dance ceaselessly? Many are those who have given their kingdom for less than solitude and the sweet fellowship of aloneness. Countless are the eagles who descend from the upper air to live with moles that they may know the secrets of the earth. There are those who renounce the kingdom of dreams that they may not seem distant from the dreamless. And those who renounce the kingdom of nakedness and cover their souls that others may not be ashamed in beholding truth uncovered and beauty unveiled. And greater yet than all of these is he who renounces the kingdom of sorrow that he may not seem proud and vainglorious."

Then rising he leaned upon his reed and said, "Go now to the great city and sit at its gate and watch all those who enter into it and those who go out. And see that you find him who, though born a king, is without kingdom; and him who though ruled in flesh rules in spirit--though neither he nor his subjects know this; and him also who but seems to rule yet is in truth slave of his own slaves."

After he had said these things he smiled on me, and there were a thousand dawns upon his lips. Then he turned and walked away into the heart of the forest.

And I returned to the city, and I sat at its gate to watch the passersby even as he had told me. And from that day to this numberless are the kings whose shadows have passed over me and few are the subjects over whom my shadow has passed.

The Lion's Daughter

Four slaves stood fanning an old queen who was asleep upon her throne. And she was snoring. And upon the queen's lap a cat lay purring and gazing lazily at the slaves.

The first slave spoke, and said, "How ugly this old woman is in her sleep. See her mouth droop; and she breathes as if the devil were choking her."

Then the cat said, purring, "Not half so ugly in her sleep as you in your waking slavery."

And the second slave said, "You would think sleep would smooth her wrinkles instead of deepening them. She must be dreaming of something evil."

And the cat purred, "Would that you might sleep also and dream of your freedom."

And the third slave said, "Perhaps she is seeing the procession of all those that she has slain."

And the cat purred, "Aye, she sees the procession of your forefathers and your descendants."

And the fourth slave said, "It is all very well to talk about her, but it does not make me less weary of standing and fanning."

And the cat purred, "You shall be fanning to all eternity; for as it is on earth so it is in heaven."

At this moment the old queen nodded in her sleep, and her crown fell to the floor.

And one of the slaves said, "That is a bad omen."

And the cat purred, "The bad omen of one is the good omen of another."

And the second slave said, "What if she should wake, and find her crown fallen! She would surely slay us."

And the cat purred, "Daily from your birth she has slain you and you know it not."

And the third slave said, "Yes, she would slay us and she would call it making sacrifice to the gods."

And the cat purred, "Only the weak are sacrificed to the gods."

And the fourth slave silenced the others, and softly he picked up the crown and replaced it, without waking her, on the old queen's head.

And the cat purred, "Only a slave restores a crown that has fallen."

And after a while the old queen woke, and she looked about her and yawned. Then she said, "Methought I dreamed, and I saw four caterpillars chased by a scorpion around the trunk of an ancient oaktree. I like not my dream."

Then she closed her eyes and went to sleep again. And she snored. And the four slaves went on fanning her.

And the cat purred, "Fan on, fan on, stupids. You fan but the fire that consumes you."

Tyranny

Thus sings the She-Dragon that guards the seven caves by the sea:

"My mate shall come riding on the waves. His thundering roar shall fill the earth with fear, and the flames of his nostrils shall set the sky afire. At the eclipse of the moon we shall be wedded, and at the eclipse of the sun I shall give birth to a Saint George, who shall slay me."

Thus sings the She-Dragon that guards the seven caves by the sea.

The Saint

In my youth I once visited a saint in his silent grove beyond the hills; and as we were conversing upon the nature of virtue a brigand came limping wearily up the ridge. When he reached the grove he knelt down before the saint and said, "O saint, I would be comforted! My sins are heavy upon me."

And the saint replied, "My sins, too, are heavy upon me."

And the brigand said, "But I am a thief and a plunderer."

And the saint replied, "I too am a thief and a plunderer."

And the brigand said, "But I am a murderer, and the blood of many men cries in my ears."

And the saint replied, "I too am a murderer, and in my ears cries the blood of many men."

And the brigand said, "I have committed countless crimes."

And the saint replied, "I too have committed crimes without number."

Then the brigand stood up and gazed at the saint, and there was a strange look in his eyes. And when he left us he went skipping down the hill.

And I turned to the saint and said, "Wherefore did you accuse yourself of uncommitted crimes? See you not that this man went away no longer believing in you?"

And the saint answered, "It is true he no longer believes in me. But he went away much comforted."

At that moment we heard the brigand singing in the distance, and the echo of his song filled the valley with gladness.

The Plutocrat

In my wanderings I once saw upon an island a man-headed, iron-hoofed monster who ate of the earth and drank of the sea incessantly. And for a long while I watched him. Then I approached him and said, "Have you never enough; is your hunger never satisfied and your thirst never quenched?"

And he answered saying, "Yes, I am satisfied, nay, I am weary of eating and drinking; but I am afraid that tomorrow there will be no more earth to eat and no more sea to drink."

The Greater Self

This came to pass. After the coronation of Nufsibaäl, King of Byblus, he retired to his bed chamber--the very room which the three hermit-magicians of the mountain had built for him. He took off his crown and his royal raiment, and stood in the centre of the room thinking of himself, now the all-powerful ruler of Byblus.

Suddenly he turned; and he saw stepping out of the silver mirror which his mother had given him, a naked man.

The king was startled, and he cried out to the man, "What would you?"

And the naked man answered, "Naught but this: Why have they crowned you king?"

And the king answered, "Because I am the noblest man in the land."

Then the naked man said, "If you were still more noble, you would not be king."

And the king said, "Because I am the mightiest man in the land they crowned me."

And the naked man said, "If you were mightier yet, you would not be king."

Then the king said, "Because I am the wisest man they crowned me king."

And the naked man said, "If you were still wiser you would not choose to be king."

Then the king fell to the floor and wept bitterly.

The naked man looked down upon him. Then he

took up the crown and with tenderness replaced it upon the king's bent head.

And the naked man, gazing lovingly upon the king, entered into the mirror.

And the king roused, and straightway he looked into the mirror. And he saw there but himself crowned.

War And The Small Nations

Once, high above a pasture, where a sheep and a lamb were grazing, an eagle was circling and gazing hungrily down upon the lamb. And as he was about to descend and seize his prey, another eagle appeared and hovered above the sheep and her young with the same hungry intent. Then the two rivals began to fight filling the sky with their fierce cries.

The sheep looked up and was much astonished. She turned to the lamb and said,

"How strange, my child, that these two noble birds should attack one another. Is not the vast sky large enough for both of them? Pray, my little one, pray in your heart that God may make peace between your winged brothers."

And the lamb prayed in his heart.

Critics

One nightfall a man travelling on horseback toward the sea reached an inn by the roadside. He dismounted, and confident in man and night like all riders toward the sea, he tied his horse to a tree beside the door and entered into the inn.

At midnight, when all were asleep, a thief came and stole the traveller's horse.

In the morning the man awoke, and discovered that his horse was stolen. And he grieved for his horse, and that a man had found it in his heart to steal.

Then his fellow-lodgers came and stood around him and began to talk.

And the first man said, "How foolish of you to tie your horse outside the stable."

And the second said, "Still more foolish, without even hobbling the horse!"

And the third man said, "It is stupid at best to travel to the sea on horseback."

And the fourth said, "Only the indolent and the slow of foot own horses."

Then the traveller was much astonished. At last he cried, "My friends, because my horse is stolen, you have hastened one and all to tell me my faults and my shortcomings. But strange, not one word of reproach have you uttered about the man who stole my horse."

Poets

Four poets were sitting around a bowl of punch that stood on a table.

Said the first poet, "Methinks I see with my third eye the fragrance of this wine hovering in space like a cloud of birds in an enchanted forest."

The second poet raised his head and said, "With my inner ear I can hear those mist-birds singing. And the melody holds my heart as the white rose imprisons the bee within her petals."

The third poet closed his eyes and stretched his arm upward, and said, "I touch them with my hand. I feel their wings, like the breath of a sleeping fairy, brushing against my fingers."

Then the fourth poet rose and lifted up the bowl, and he said, "Alas, friends! I am too dull of sight and of hearing and of touch. I cannot see the fragrance of this wine, nor hear its song, nor feel the beating of its wings. I perceive but the wine itself. Now therefore must I drink it, that it may sharpen my senses and raise me to your blissful heights."

And putting the bowl to his lips, he drank the punch to the very last drop.

The three poets, with their mouths open, looked at him aghast, and there was a thirsty yet unlyrical hatred in their eyes.

The Weather-Cock

Said the weather-cock to the wind, "How tedious and monotonous you are! Can you not blow any other way but in my face? You disturb my God-given stability."

And the wind did not answer. It only laughed in space.

The King Of Aradus

Once the elders of the city of Aradus presented themselves before the king, and besought of him a decree to forbid to men all wine and all intoxicants within their city.

And the king turned his back upon them and went out from them laughing.

Then the elders departed in dismay.

At the door of the palace they met the lord chamberlain. And the lord chamberlain observed that they were troubled, and he understood their case.

Then he said, "Pity, my friends! Had you found the king drunk, surely he would have granted you your petition."

Out Of My Deeper Heart

Out of my deeper heart a bird rose and flew skyward. Higher and higher did it rise, yet larger and larger did it grow.

At first it was but like a swallow, then a lark, then an eagle, then as vast as a spring cloud, and then it filled the starry heavens.

Out of my heart a bird flew skyward. And it waxed larger as it flew. Yet it left not my heart.

*

O my faith, my untamed knowledge, how shall I fly to your height and see with you man's larger self pencilled upon the sky?

How shall I turn this sea within me into mist, and move with you in space immeasurable?

How can a prisoner within the temple behold its golden domes?

How shall the heart of a fruit be stretched to envelop the fruit also?

O my faith, I am in chains behind these bars of silver and ebony, and I cannot fly with you.

Yet out of my heart you rise skyward, and it is my heart that holds you, and I shall be content.

Dynasties

The Queen of Ishana was in travail of childbirth; and the King and the mighty men of his court were waiting in breathless anxiety in the great hall of the Winged Bulls.

At eventide there came suddenly a messenger in haste and prostrated himself before the King, and said, "I bring glad tidings unto my lord the King, and unto the kingdom and the slaves of the King. Mihrab the Cruel, thy life-long enemy, the King of Bethroun, is dead."

When the King and the mighty men heard this, they all rose and shouted for joy; for the powerful Mihrab, had he lived longer, had assuredly overcome Ishana and carried the inhabitants captive.

At this moment the court physician also entered the hall of Winged Bulls, and behind him came the royal midwives. And the physician prostrated himself before the king, and said, "My lord the King shall live for ever, and through countless generations shall he rule over the people of Ishana. For unto thee, O King, is born this very hour a son, who shall be thy heir."

Then indeed was the soul of the King intoxicated with joy, that in the same moment his foe was dead and the royal line was established.

Now in the City of Ishana lived a true prophet. And the prophet was young, and bold of spirit. And the King that very night ordered that the prophet should be brought before him. And when he was brought, the King said unto him, "Prophesy now, and foretell what shall be the future of my son who is this day born unto the kingdom."

And the prophet hesitated not, but said, "Hearken, O King, and I will indeed prophesy of the future of thy son, that is this day born. The soul of thy enemy, even of thy enemy King Mihrab, who died yestereve, lingered but a day upon the wind. Then it sought for itself a body to enter into. And that which it entered into was the body of thy son that, is born unto thee this hour."

Then the King was enraged, and with his sword he slew the prophet.

And from that day to this, the wise men of Ishana say one to another secretly, "Is it not known, and has it not been said from of old, that Ishana is ruled by an enemy."

Knowledge And Half-Knowledge

Four frogs sat upon a log that lay floating on the edge of a river. Suddenly the log was caught by the current and swept slowly down the stream. The frogs were delighted and absorbed, for never before had they sailed.

At length the first frog spoke, and said, "This is indeed a most marvellous log. It moves as if alive. No such log was ever known before."

Then the second frog spoke, and said, "Nay, my friend, the log is like other logs, and does not move. It is the river, that is walking to the sea, and carries us and the log with it."

And the third frog spoke, and said, "It is neither the log nor the river that moves. The moving is in our thinking. For without thought nothing moves."

And the three frogs began to wrangle about what was really moving. The quarrel grew hotter and louder, but they could not agree.

Then they turned to the fourth frog, who up to this time had been listening attentively but holding his peace, and they asked his opinion.

And the fourth frog said, "Each of you is right, and none of you is wrong. The moving is in the log and the water and our thinking also."

And the three frogs became very angry, for none of

them was willing to admit that his was not the whole truth, and that the other two were not wholly wrong.

Then the strange thing happened. The three frogs got together and pushed the fourth frog off the log into the river.

"Said A Sheet of Snow-White Paper...."

Said a sheet of snow-white paper, "Pure was I created, and pure will I remain for ever. I would rather be burnt and turn to white ashes than suffer darkness to touch me or the unclean to come near me."

The ink-bottle heard what the paper was saying, and it laughed in its dark heart; but it never dared to approach her. And the multicoloured pencils heard her also, and they too never came near her.

And the snow-white sheet of paper did remain pure and chaste for ever--pure and chaste--and empty.

The Scholar And The Poet

Said the serpent to the lark, "Thou flyest, yet thou canst not visit the recesses of the earth where the sap of life moveth in perfect silence."

And the lark answered, "Aye, thou knowest over much, nay thou art wiser than all things wise--pity thou canst not fly."

And as if he did not hear, the serpent said, "Thou canst not see the secrets of the deep, nor move among the treasures of the hidden empire. It was but yesterday I lay in a cave of rubies. It is like the heart of a ripe pomegranate, and the faintest ray of light turns it into a flame-rose. Who but me can behold such marvels?"

And the lark said, "None, none but thee can lie among the crystal memories of the cycles: pity thou canst not sing."

And the serpent said, "I know a plant whose root descends to the bowels of the earth, and he who eats of that root becomes fairer than Ashtarte."

And the lark said, "No one, no one but thee could unveil the magic thought of the earth--pity thou canst not fly."

And the serpent said, "There is a purple stream that runneth under a mountain, and he who drinketh of it shall become immortal even as the gods. Surely no bird or beast can discover that purple stream."

And the lark answered, "If thou willest thou canst become deathless even as the gods--pity thou canst not sing."

And the serpent said, "I know a buried temple, which I visit once a moon: It was built by a forgotten race of giants, and upon its walls are graven the secrets of time and space, and he who reads them shall understand that which passeth all understanding."

And the lark said, "Verily, if thou so desirest thou canst encircle with thy pliant body all knowledge of time and space--pity thou canst not fly."

Then the serpent was disgusted, and as he turned and entered into his hole he muttered, "Empty headed songster!"

And the lark flew away singing, "Pity thou canst not sing. Pity, pity, my wise one, thou canst not fly."

Values

Once a man unearthed in his field a marble statue of great beauty. And he took it to a collector who loved all beautiful things and offered it to him for sale, and the collector bought it for a large price. And they parted.

And as the man walked home with his money he thought, and he said to himself, "How much life this money means! How can any one give all this for a dead carved stone buried and undreamed of in the earth for a thousand years?"

And now the collector was looking at his statue, and he was thinking, and he said to himself, "What beauty! What life! The dream of what a soul!--and fresh with the sweet sleep of a thousand years. How can any one give all this for money, dead and dreamless?"

Other Seas

A fish said to another fish, "Above this sea of ours there is another sea, with creatures swimming in it--and they live there even as we live here."

The fish replied, "Pure fancy! Pure fancy! When you know that everything that leaves our sea by even an inch, and stays out of it, dies. What proof have you of other lives in other seas?"

Repentance

On a moonless night a man entered into his neighbour's garden and stole the largest melon he could find and brought it home.

He opened it and found it still unripe.

Then behold a marvel!

The man's conscience woke and smote him with remorse; and he repented having stolen the melon.

The Dying Man And The Vulture

Wait, wait yet awhile, my eager friend.
I shall yield but too soon this wasted thing,
Whose agony overwrought and useless
Exhausts your patience.
I would not have your honest hunger
Wait upon these moments:
But this chain, though made of a breath,
Is hard to break. And the will to die,
Stronger than all things strong,
Is stayed by a will to live
Feebler than all things feeble.
Forgive me comrade;
I tarry too long.
It is memory that holds my spirit;
A procession of distant days,
A vision of youth spent in a dream,
A face that bids my eyelids not to sleep,
A voice that lingers in my ears,
A hand that touches my hand.
Forgive me that you have waited too long.
It is over now, and all is faded:--
The face, the voice, the hand and the mist that brought them hither.
The knot is untied.
The cord is cleaved.
And that which is neither food nor drink is withdrawn.
Approach, my hungry comrade;
The board is made ready,
And the fare, frugal and spare,
Is given with love.
Come, and dig your beak here, into the left side,

And tear out of its cage this smaller bird,
Whose wings can beat no more:
I would have it soar with you into the sky.
Come now, my friend, I am your host tonight,
And you my welcome guest.

Beyond My Solitude

Beyond my solitude is another solitude, and to him who dwells therein my aloneness is a crowded market-place and my silence a confusion of sounds.

Too young am I and too restless to seek that above-solitude. The voices of yonder valley still hold my ears, and its shadows bar my way and I cannot go.

Beyond these hills is a grove of enchantment and to him who dwells therein my peace is but a whirlwind and my enchantment an illusion.

Too young am I and too riotous to seek that sacred grove. The taste of blood is clinging in my mouth, and the bow and the arrows of my fathers yet linger in my hand and I cannot go.

Beyond this burdened self lives my freer self; and to him my dreams are a battle fought in twilight and my desires the rattling of bones.

Too young am I and too outraged to be my freer self.

And how shall I become my freer self unless I slay my burdened selves, or unless all men become free?

How shall my leaves fly singing upon the wind unless my roots shall wither in the dark?

How shall the eagle in me soar against the sun until my fledglings leave the nest which I with my own beak have built for them?

The Last Watch

At the high-tide of night, when the first breath of dawn came upon the wind, the Forerunner, he who calls himself echo to a voice yet unheard, left his bed-chamber and ascended to the roof of his house. Long he stood and looked down upon the slumbering city. Then he raised his head, and even as if the sleepless spirits of all those asleep had gathered around him, he opened his lips and spoke, and he said:

"My friends and my neighbours and you who daily pass my gate, I would speak to you in your sleep, and in the valley of your dreams I would walk naked and unrestrained; far heedless are your waking hours and deaf are your sound-burdened ears.

"Long did I love you and overmuch.

"I love the one among you as though he were all, and all as if you were one. And in the spring of my heart I sang in your gardens, and in the summer of my heart I watched at your threshing-floors.

"Yea, I loved you all, the giant and the pigmy, the leper and the anointed, and him who gropes in the dark even as him who dances his days upon the mountains.

"You, the strong, have I loved, though the marks of your iron hoofs are yet upon my flesh; and you the weak, though you have drained my faith and wasted my patience.

"You the rich have I loved, while bitter was your honey to my mouth; and you the poor, though you knew my empty-handed shame.

"You the poet with the barrowed lute and blind fingers, you have I loved in self indulgence; and you the scholar, ever gathering rotted shrouds in potters' fields.

"You the priest I have loved, who sit in the silences of yesterday questioning the fate of my tomorrow; and you the worshippers of gods the images of your own desires.

"You the thirsting woman whose cup is ever full, I have loved you in understanding; and you the woman of restless nights, you too I have loved in pity.

"You the talkative have I loved, saying, 'Life hath much to say'; and you the dumb have I loved, whispering to myself, 'Says he not in silence that which I fain would hear in words?'

"And you the judge and the critic, I have loved also; yet when you have seen me crucified, you said, 'He bleeds rhythmically, and the pattern his blood makes upon his white skin is beautiful to behold.'

"Yea, I have loved you all, the young and the old, the trembling reed and the oak.

"But alas! it was the over-abundance of my heart that turned you from me. You would drink love from a cup, but not from a surging river. You would hear love's faint murmur, but when love shouts you would muffle your ears.

"And because I have loved you all you have said, 'Too soft and yielding is his heart, and too undiscerning is his path. It is the love of a needy one, who picks crumbs even as he sits at kingly feasts. And it is the love of a weakling, for the strong loves only the strong.'

"And because I have loved you overmuch you have

said, 'It is but the love of a blind man who knows not the beauty of one nor the ugliness of another. And it is the love of the tasteless who drinks vinegar even as wine. And it is the love of the impertinent and the overweening, for what stranger could be our mother and father and sister and brother?'

"This you have said, and more. For often in the marketplace you pointed your fingers at me and said mockingly, 'There goes the ageless one, the man without seasons, who at the noon hour plays games with our children and at eventide sits with our elders and assumes wisdom and understanding.'

"And I said 'I will love them more. Aye, even more. I will hide my love with seeming to hate, and disguise my tenderness as bitterness. I will wear an iron mask, and only when armed and mailed shall I seek them.'

"Then I laid a heavy hand upon your bruises, and like a tempest in the night I thundered in your ears.

"From the housetop I proclaimed you hypocrites, pharisees, tricksters, false and empty earth-bubbles.

"The short-sighted among you I cursed for blind bats, and those too near the earth I likened to soulless moles.

"The eloquent I pronounced fork-tongued, the silent, stone-lipped, and the simple and artless I called the dead never weary of death.

"The seekers after world knowledge I condemned as offenders of the holy spirit and those who would naught but the spirit I branded as hunters of shadows who cast their nets in flat waters and catch but their own images.

"Thus with my lips have I denounced you, while my heart, bleeding within me, called you tender names.

"It was love lashed by its own self that spoke. It was pride half slain that fluttered in the dust. It was my hunger for your love that raged from the housetop, while my own love, kneeling in silence, prayed your forgiveness.

"But behold a miracle!

"It was my disguise that opened your eyes, and my seeming to hate that woke your hearts.

"And now you love me.

"You love the swords that strike you and the arrows that crave your breast. For it comforts you to be wounded and only when you drink of your own blood can you be intoxicated.

"Like moths that seek destruction in the flame you gather daily in my garden: and with faces uplifted and eyes enchanted you watch me tear the fabric of your days. And in whispers you say the one to the other, 'He sees with the light of God. He speaks like the prophets of old. He unveils our souls and unlocks our hearts, and like the eagle that knows the way of foxes he knows our ways.'

"Aye, in truth, I know your ways, but only as an eagle knows the ways of his fledglings. And I fain would disclose my secret. Yet in my need for your nearness I feign remoteness, and in fear of the ebbtide of your love I guard the floodgates of my love."

After saying these things the Forerunner covered his face with his hands and wept bitterly. For he knew in his heart that love humiliated in its nakedness is greater than love that seeks triumph in disguise; and he was ashamed.

But suddenly he raised his head, and like one waking from sleep he outstretched his arms and said, "Night is over, and we children of night must die when dawn comes leaping upon the hills; and out of our ashes a mightier love shall rise. And it shall laugh in the sun, and it shall be deathless."

PROSE POEMS

At The Door Of The Temple

I purified my lips with the sacred fire to
 speak of love,
But when I opened my lips I found myself
 speechless.
Before I knew love, I was went to chant
 the songs of love,
But when I learned to know, the words
in my mouth became naught save
 breath,
And the tunes within my breast fell into
 deep silence.
In the past, when you would question me
 concerning the secrets and the mysteries of love.
I would speak and answer you with assurance.
But now that love has adorned me with vestments,
I come, in my turn, to question you of all
 the ways of love, and all its wonders.
Who among you can answer me?
I come to question you about my self and
 that which is in me.
Who among you can reveal my self?
Tell me now, what flame is this that burns
 within my bosom,
Consuming my strength, and melting my
 hopes and my desires?
What hands are these, light, gentle, and
 alluring.

Which enfold my spirit in its hours of
    loneliness
And pour into the vessel of my heart a
    wine mixed of the bitterness of joy
And the sweetness of pain?
What wings are these beating around my
    bed in the long silence of the night,
So that I am wakeful, watching- I know
    not what;
Listening to that I do not hear, and gazing
    upon that I do not see;
Meditating on that I do not comprehend,
    and possessing that I have not attained.
Ay, wakeful am I, sighing,
For to me sighs and griefs are lovelier that
    the right of joy and laughter;
Wakeful am I in the hand of an unseen
    power that slay me and then quickens me,
Even until the day dawns and fills the
    corners of my house with light.
Then do I sleep, while between my withered
    eyelids the shadows of my wake-
    fulness still quiver,
And above my bed of stone hovers the
    figure of a dream.

....

And what is this that we call love?
Tell me, what is this mystic secret hiding
    behind the semblance of our life,
And living in the heart of our existence?
What is this vast release coming as a cause
    to all effects, and as an effect unto all causes?

What is this quickening that gathers death
　　　and life and from them creates a dream
More strange than life, and deeper far
　　　than death?
Tell me, my brothers, tell me, which of
　　　you would not awake from this sleep
　　　of life
When your spirit feels the touch of love's
　　　white fingers?
Which of you would not forsake his father
　　　and his mother and his birthplace
When the maiden his heart loves calls our
　　　to him?
Which of you would not cross the desert
　　　and climb the mountain and sail the seas
To seek her to whom your spirit yearns?
What youth, indeed, would not follow to
　　　the earth's uttermost bounds,
If one awaits him there whose breath and
　　　voice and touch he shall find sweet
　　　and wholesome?
What man would not thus burn his soul
　　　as incense
Before a god who regards his craving and
　　　grants him his petition?
　　　　　　　........
It was but yesterday that I stood at the
　　　door of the temple
Questioning the passers-by concerning
　　　the mysteries and the benefits of love.
And a man passed by, of middle age,
　　　wasted and with a scowling
　　　countenance, and he said:

"Love is an inborn weakness which we
	have inherited from the first man."
Then a youth, strong and stalwart of body
	and arm, came chanting:
"Love is a resolution which accompanies
	our being, and binds this present
	with the ages past and future."
And now a sad-faced woman, passing,
	sighed and said:
"Love is a deadly venom which dark and
	fearful vipers diffuse in space from
	the abyss of hell,
So that it descends in dew upon the thirsty
	soul,
And the soul therefrom becomes for a
	moment drunken, then sobered for a
	year, and dead an aeon."
But a young maiden, rosy, and with
	laughing lips, said:
"See, love is a nectar which the brides of
	dawn pour for the strong
So that they rise glorified before the stars
	of night, and joyous before the sun of day."
Thereafter came a man in a garment of
	sombre black , and a loose bread that
	fell upon his breast, and he said sternly:
"Love is a stupidity which comes with the
	dawn of youth and is gone with its
	eventide."
And one followed him with face radiant
	and serene, saying in tranquil joy:
"Love is a heavenly wisdom that lights
	our inner and outer eye

So that we may behold all things even as
   the gods."
Then passed by a blind man questioning
   the ground with his old staff, and
   there was a wailing in his voice as
   he said:
"Love is a dense fog to enshroud the
   soul, and veil from it the shows of
   life.
So that the soul sees naught but the shadows
   of its desires
Lost among rocky steeps,
And hears naught but the echo of its voice
   shouting from the valleys of desolation."
Then passed by a young man playing upon
   a lyre and singing;
"Love is a celestial light shining from the
   innermost of the sensitive self to
   illumine all about it,
That it may behold the worlds as a procession
   moving in green meadows,
And life as a dream of beauty between
   awakening and awakening."
And after the young man followed one
   decrepit, and with dragging feet, trembling,
   and he said:
"Love is the repose of the sad body in the silent grave,
And it is the security of the soul in the
   fastnesses of eternity."
Then came a young child whose years
   were but five, and he ran and
   shouted:
"Love is my father, and love is my mother,

And no one knows of love but my mother
     and my father."

     ....

And now the day was done and all the
     people were passed by before the temple,
And each and every one had spoken of love,
And in each word he had revealed his own
     longing and desire
And had disclosed the secret mysteries of
     life.
When evening was fully come, and the
     moving through had gone their ways,
And all was hushed,
I heard a voice within the temple saying:
"All life is twain, the one a frozen stream,
     the other a burning flame,
And the burning flame is love".
Thereupon I entered into the temple and
     bowed myself, kneeling in supplication
And chanting a prayer in my secret heat:
"Make me, O Lord, food for the burning
     flame,
And make me, O God, fuel for the sacred
     fire,
Amen."

Revelation

When the night waxed deep and slumber
    cast its cloak upon the face of the earth,
I left my bed and sought the sea, saying
    to myself:
"The sea never sleeps, and the wakefulness
    of the sea brings comfort to a sleepless soul."
When I reached the shore, the mist had
    already descended from the
    mountains tops
And covered the world as a veil adorns the
    face of a maiden.
There I stood gazing at the waves, listening
    to their sighing and considering
    the power that lies behind them-
The power that travels with the storm,
    and rages with the volcano, that
    smiles with smiling flowers and
    makes melody with murmuring
    brooks.
After a while I turned, and lo,
I beheld three figures sitting upon a rock
    near by,
And I saw that the mist veiled them, and
    yet it veiled them not.
Slowly I walked toward the rock whereon
    they sat, drawn by some power which
    I know not.
A few paces off I stood and gazed upon
    them, for there was magic in the place

Which crystallized my purpose and
    bestirred my fancy.
And at that moment one of the three arose,
    and with a voice that seemed to come
    from the sea depths he said:
"Life without love is like a tree without
    blossoms or fruit.
And love without beauty is like flowers
    without fragrance, and fruit without
    seeds.
Life, Love, and Beauty are three entities
    in one self, free and boundless,
Which know neither change nor separation."
This he said, and sat again in his place.
Then the second figure arose, and with a
    voice like the roar of rushing waters
    he said:
"Life without rebellion is like the seasons
    without a spring.
And rebellion without right is like spring
    in an arid and barren desert.
Life, Rebellion, and Right are three
    entities in one self,
And in them is neither change nor separation;"
This he said, and sat again in his place.
Then the third figure arose, and spoke
    with a voice like the peal of the thunder,
    saying:
"Life without freedom is like a body
    without a spirit.
And freedom without thought is like a
    spirit confounded.
Life, Freedom, and Thought are three

       entities in one eternal self,
Which neither vanish nor pass away."
Then the three arose and with voices of
       majesty and awe they spoke:
"Love and all that it begets,
Rebellion and all that it creates,
Freedom and all that it generates,
These three are aspects of God...
And God is the infinite mind of the finite
       and conscious world."
Then silence followed, filled with the stirring
       of invisible wings and the tremor
       of the ethereal bodies.
And I closed my eyes, listening to the echo
       of the saying which I heard.
When I opened my eyes, I beheld naught
       but the sea hidden beneath a blanket
       of mist:
And I moved closer toward that rock
And I beheld naught but a pillar of incense
       rising unto the sky.

The Soul

........And the God of Gods created the
        soul, fashioning it for beauty.
He gave unto it the gentleness of a breeze
        at dawn, the scent of flowers, the
        loveliness of moonlight.
He gave unto it also the cup of joy,
        and He said:
"You shall not drink of this cup save that
        you have forgotten the past and
        renounced the future."
He gave unto it also the cup of sorrow,
        saying:
"Drink that you may understand the
        meaning of joy."
Then God bestowed within the soul love
        that would depart with the first sigh
        of content,
And sweetness that would free from the
        first word of arrogance.
He made a heavenly sign to guide it in the
        path of truth.
He placed in its depths an eye that would
        behold the unseen.
He created within it a fancy to flow like a
        river with phantoms and moving figures.
He clothed it in garments of longing
        woven by angels, from the rainbow.
Within it He placed also the darkness of
        bewilderment, which is the shadow
        of light.

And God took fire from the forge of anger,
Wind blowing from the desert of ignorance;
Sand He gathered from the seashore of
    selffulness
And dust from beneath the feet of the ages;
Thus He fashioned man.
And unto man He gave blind strength that
    leaps into a flame in moments of mad
    passion, and lies down before desire.
God gave him life which is the shadow of
    death.
And the God of Gods smiled and wept,
    and He knew a love which hath no
    bound nor end;
Thus He united man and his soul.

Song Of The Night

The night is hushed,
And the dreams hide in silence.
The moon is rising -
She has eyes to watch the day.
Come, daughter of the fields,
And let us go
Into the vineyards
Where the lovers meet.
For it may be
That there we, too, may quench
With love's good vintage
The drouth of our desire.
Hearken, the nightingale
Pours forth his song
Into the valleys
Which the hills have filled
With the green scent of mint.
Fear not, beloved,
The stars will keep the secret of our meeting,
And the soft mist of night
Veil our embrace.
Fear not -
The young bride of the djinns
In her enchanted cave
Lies sleeping, drunk with love,
And well-nigh hidden
From the houris eyes.

And even should the king of the djinns
Pass by,
Then love will turn him back.
For is he not a lover as I am,
And shall he disclose
That which his own heart suffers?

My Soul Counselled Me

My soul spoke unto me and counseled me
    To love all that others hate,
And to befriend those whom others defame.
My soul counseled me and revealed unto
    Me that love dignifies not alone the
    One who lovers, but also the beloved.
Unto that day love was for me a thread of
    Cobweb between two flowers, close
To one another;
But now it has become a halo with neither
Beginning nor end,
Encircling all that has been and waxing
    Eternally to embrace all that shall be.
        x x x
My soul counseled me and taught me to
    See beauty veiled by form and colour.
My soul charged me to gaze steadfastly
    Upon all that is deemed ugly until it
    Appears lovely.
Before my soul had thus charged and
    Counseled me,
I had seemed to see beauty like unto wavering
    torches between pillars of smoke;
But now the smoke has dispersed and
    vanished and I see naught but the burning.
        x x x
My soul counseled me and charged me to
    listen for voices that rise neither from
    the tongue nor the throat.

Before that day I heard but dully, and
> Naught save clamour and loud cries
> Came to my ears;
But now I have learned to listen to silence,
To hear its Choirs singing the songs of ages,
Chanting the hymns of space, and disclosing
> the secrets of eternity.

x x x

My soul spoke unto me and counseled me
> to quench my thirst with that wine
> which may not be poured into cups,
Nor lifted by hands, nor touched by lips.
Unto that day my thirst was like a dim
> spark laid in ashes
To be put out by a draught from any spring;
But now my strong yearning has become
> my cup,
Love has become my wine, and loneliness
> my joy.

x x x

My soul counseled me and charged me to
> seek that which is unseen;
And my soul revealed unto me that the
> thing we grasp is the thing we desire.
In other days I was content with warmth
> in winter, and with a cooling zephyr
> in the summer season;
But now my fingers are become as mist,
Letting fall all that they have held, to mingle
> with the unseen that I now desire.

x x x

My soul spoke to me and invited me to
> breathe the fragrance from a plant

That has neither root nor stalk nor blossom,
and that to eye has seen.
Before my soul counseled me thus, I
sought perfumers in the gardens,
In jars of sweet-smelling herbs and vessels
   of incense;
But now I am aware only of an incense
   that may not be burned,
I breathe an air more fragrant than all
   earth's gardens and all the winds of space.

x x x

My soul counseled me and charged me to
   answer and say; "I follow", when
   the unknown and the adventurous
   call unto me.
Hitherto I had answered naught but the
   voice of the crier in the market-place,
Nor did I purpose aught save toads charted
   and well trodden;
But now the known has become a steed
   that I mount to seek the unknown,
And the road has become a ladder by
   which I may climb to the perilous
summit.
My soul counseled me and admonished
   me to measure time with this saying :
"There was a yesterday and there shall
   be a tomorrow."
Unto that hour I deemed the past an epoch
   that is lost and shall be forgotten,
And the future I deemed an era that I may
   not attain;
But now I have learned this :

That in the brief present all time, with all
    That is in time,
Is achieved and come true.

x x x

My soul spoke and revealed unto me that
    I am not bound in space by the words:
"Here, there, and over there."
Hitherto I stood upon my hill, and every
    other hill seemed distant and far
    away;
But now I know that the hill whereon I
    dwell is indeed all hills,
And the valley whereunto I descend comprehends all valleys.
My soul counseled me and besought me
    to watch while others sleep
And to seek my pillow while they are
    wakeful,
For in all my years I had not perceived
    their dreams, nor they mine.
But now I am winged by day in my dreaming,
And when they sleep I behold them free
    upon the night,
And I rejoice in their freedom.

x x x

My soul counseled me and charged me
    lest I be exalted because of overpraise
And lest I be distressed for fear of blame.
Until that day I doubted the worth of my
    own handiwork;
But now I have learned this:
That the trees blossom in spring, and bear
    fruit in summer,

And drop their leaves in autumn to become
       utterly naked in winter
Without exaltation and without fear of
       shame.
My soul counseled me and assured me
That I am neither higher than the pygmy
       nor lower than the giant.
Before that day I beheld mankind as two
       men,
The one a weakling whom I derided or
       pitied,
And the other a mighty man whom I would
       either follow, or oppose in rebellion.
But now I know that I was formed even
       from the same dust of which all men
       are created,
That my elements are their elements, and
       my inner self is their inner self.
My struggle is their struggle, and their
       pilgrimage is mine own.
If they transgress, I am also the transgressor,
And if they do well, then I have a share in
       their well-doing,
If they arise, I too arise with them; if they
       Stay behind, I also, to company them.

             x x x

My soul counseled me and instructed me
       to see that the light which I carry is
       not my light,
That my song was not created within me;
For though I travel with the light, I am
       not the light,

And though I am a lute fastened with
      strings,
I am not the lute-player.

x x x

My soul counseled me, my brother, and
      enlightened me.
And oftentimes has your soul counseled
      and enlightened you.
For you are like me, and there is no
difference between us
Save that I speak of what is within me in
      words that I have heard in my silence,
And you guard what is within you, and
      your guardianship is as goodly as my
      much speaking.

My Birthday
(Written while studying art in Partis, January 6, 1908)

On the day my mother gave me birth,
On that day five-and-twenty years ago,
Silence placed me in the vast hands of life,
    Abounding with struggle and conflict.
Lo, five-and-twenty times have I jour
    neyed round the sun.
How many times the moon has journeyed
    round me I do not know.
But this I know, that I have not yet
    learned the secrets of light,
Nor have I understood the mysteries of
    darkness.
Five-and-twenty times have I journeyed
    with the earth, the moon, the sun and
    stars encircling the universe.
Lo, not my soul whispers the names of
    cosmic systems
Even as the caverns of the sea resound to
    the waves,
For the soul exists, a current in the cos-
    mos, but does not know is power.
And the soul chants the cosmic rhythm,
    high and low,
Yet attains not the fullness of its harmonies.
Five-and-twenty years ago Time wrote me
    down in the book of this strange and
    awful life.

Lo, a word am I, signifying now nothing
       and now many things.
On that day of every year what thoughts
       and what memories throng my
       soul !
They halt before me - the procession of
       the days gone by.
The parade of the phantoms of the
       night -
Then are they swept away, even as the
       wind sweeps clouds from the horizon;
They vanish in the darkness of my house
       as the songs of the rivulets in desolate
       and distant valleys.
On that day, every year, those spirits
       which have shaped my spirit
Come seeking me from the far ends of the
       worlds,
And chanting words of sorrowful remembrance.
Then they are gone, to hide behind the
       semblance of this life,
Even as birds descending to a threshing-
       floor and finding no seeds to feast
       upon,
Hover but a moment and fly hence to seek
       Another place.
Ever upon that day the meanings of my
       past life stand before me, like dim
       mirrors
Wherein I look for a while and see naught
       but the pallid corpse-like faces of the
       years,

Naught but the wrinkled and aged visages
       of hopes and dreams long lost.
Once more I look upon those mirrors, and
       there behold only my own still face.
I gaze thereon beholding naught but sadness.
I question sadness and I find it has no
       speech;
Yet could sadness speak, methinks it
       would utter a sweeter word than joy.
For five-and-twenty years I have loved
       much,
And oftentimes have I loved what others
       hate.
Yet what I loved as a child I love now,
And what I now love I shall love unto the
       end of life;
For love is all I have, and none shall make
       me lose it.
Oftentimes have I loved death,
Called death sweet names and spoken of
       it in loving words both openly and
       secretly.
Yet though I have not forgotten, nor
       broken the vows of death,
I have learned to love life also.
For death and life have become equal to
       me in beauty and in joy;
They have shared in the growth of my
       yearning and desire,
And they have divided my love and
       tenderness.
Freedom also have I loved, even as life and
       death.

And as my love grew, so grew also my
    knowledge of men's slavery to
    tyranny and contempt,
The while I beheld their submission to
    idols hewn by the dark ages,
Reared in ignorance and polished by the
    lips of slaves.
But I loved these slaves as I loved freedom
    and I pitied them, for they are
blind men
Kissing the jaws of foul bloodthirsty
    beasts, and seeing not;
Sucking the venom of malignant vipers,
    and feeling not;
Digging their graves with their own hands,
    and knowing not.
Freedom have I loved more than aught else,
For I have found freedom like unto a
    maiden wasted from privation and
    seclusion.
Till she became a ghost that moves
    among the house in the lonely
    streets,
And when she calls out to the passers-by,
    they neither hear nor look.
Like all men, during these five-and-twenty
    years I have loved happiness;
I have learned to awake at every dawn and
    seek it, even as they.
But never have I found it in their ways,
Nor seen the trace of the footsteps of
    happiness on the sand near their
    mansions,

Nor have I heard the echo of its voice from
    the windows of their temples.
I sought alone to find it.
I heard my soul whisper in my ear:
"Happiness is a maiden born and reared
    In the fastness of the heart;
She comes never from beyond its walls."
Yet when I opened the portal of my heart
    to find happiness,
I saw therein her mirror and her bed and
    her garments, but herself I could
    not find.
Mankind have I loved. Ay, much have I
    loved men,
And men in my opinion are three:
The one who curse life, the one who
    blesses it, and the one who
contemplates it.
The first I have loved for his misery, the
    second for his beneficence, and the
    third for his wisdom.

x x x

Thus passed the five-and-twenty years,
And thus my days and nights, pursuing
    each other down my life
As the leaves of trees scatter before the
    winds of autumn.
And today I pause remembering, even as
    a weary climber half-way to the
    summit,
And I look backward, and to right and
    left, but I see no treasure any-
    where

Which I may claim and say: "This is
        mine own."
Nor do I find in the seasons of my years
        any harvest
Save only sheets of fair white paper traced
        over with marking of black ink,
And strange and fragmentary canvases
        filled in with lines and colours, both
        harmonious and inharmonious.
In these have I shrouded and buried the
        loveliness and the freedom that I
        have thought and dreamed,
Even as the ploughman who goes to the
        field to sow his seeds in furrows
Returns to his house at eventide hoping
        and waiting.
But I, though I have sowed well the seeds
        of my heart,
Yet I have neither hoped nor waited.
And now that I have reached this season
        of my life,
The past seems hidden behind a mist of
        sighs and grief,
And the future revealed through the veil
        of the past.
I pause and gaze at life from my small
        window;
I behold the faces of men, and I hear their
        shouting rise into the sky.
I heed their footsteps falling among the
        streets of houses,
And I perceive the communion of their
        spirits, the eagerness of their desires,

   the yearning of their hearts.
I pause and behold the children throwing
   dust upon each other with laughter
   and loud cries.
I behold boys with their faces upward
   lifted as though they were reading
   an ode to youth written upon the
   margins of a cloud
Lined with the gleaming radiance of the sun.
I behold young maidens swaying to and
   fro, like branches of a tree,
Smiling like flowers, and gazing at the
   youths from behind eyelids
Quivering with love and soft desire.
I behold the aged walking slowly, with
   their low-bent backs,
Leaning upon their staffs and gazing
   fixedly at the earth
As if their old dim eyes were searching in
   the dust for lost bright jewels.
I pause beside my window and I gaze at
   all these shapes and shadows
Moving and creeping silently about the city.
Then I look after beyond the city to the
   wilderness,
And I behold all that is therein of dreadful
   beauty and of calling silence,
Its lofty mounds and little valleys, its
   springing trees and tremulous
   grasses,
Its flowers with perfume laden, and its
whispering rivers,

Its wild birds singing, and all its humming
      winged life.
I gaze beyond the wilderness, and there,
      behold, the ocean -
With its deep wonders and mysterious
      secrets, its hid treasures;
There I behold all that is upon the face of
      the ranging, rushing, foaming waters
And the spray that rises and the vapours
      that descend.
I peer far beyond the ocean and behold
      the infinity of space,
The drifting worlds, the glimmering
constellations, the suns and moons,
the fixed and the shooting stars;
And I behold the evidence of forces for-
      ever attracting and repelling, the
      wars of elements, creating, changing,
      and withal held prisoner within a law
      of no beginning and no end.
These things I contemplate through my
      small window, and I forget my five-
      and-twenty years,
And all the centuries which have preceded
      them,
And all the ages that shall follow.
Then my life, with its revelations and its
      mysteries, seems to me like the
      sighing of a child
That trembles in the void of the eternal
      depths and heights.
Yet this atom, this self that I call /, makes
      ever a stirring and a clamour,

Lifting its wings towards the four corners
 of the earth,
Its being poised upon the point of time
 which gave it conscious life.
Then from the holy of where this
 living spark abides, a voice arises
 crying:
"Peace be with you, life !
Peace be with you, awakening !
Peace be with you, realization !
Peace be with you, day, whose abundant
 light enfolds the darkness of earth !
Peace be with you, night, whose darkness
 reveals the light of heaven !
Peace be with you, seasons !
Peace be with you, spring, that renews the
 youth of the earth !
Peace be with you, summer, that enriches
 the glory of the sun !
Peace be with you, summer, that bestows
 the fruits of labour and the harvest
 of toil !
Peace be with you, winter, that restores
 with tempests the wasted strength
of nature !
Peace be with you, years, which disclose
 What the years have hidden !
Peace be with you, ages, which disclose
 what the years have hidden !
Peace be with you, ages, which restore
 what the centuries have destroyed !
Peace be with you, time, which moves
 with us unto the perfect day !

Peace be with you, spirit, that guards with
        prudence the reins of life, hidden
        from us by the sun !
Peace be with you, heart, that you are
        moved to acclaim peace
The while you bathe in tears !
Peace be with you, lips, that you utter
        peace
The while you taste the bread of bitterness !"

Be Still, My Heart

Be still, my heart. Space does not hear you.
Be still, my heart. The ether, heavy with
 mourning and with lamentation, will
 not bear your songs.
Be still, for the phantoms of night will not
 heed the whisper of your mysteries,
And the procession of darkness will not
 halt before your dreams.
Be still, my heart, be still until dawn.
For whoso waits the morning patiently
 will greet the morning with strength,
And whoso loves the light, by light shall he
 be loved.
Be still, my heart, and listen to my words.
In dreams I heard a blackbird singing
 above the mouth of a raging volcano,
And saw a lily lifting its head above the
snow;
I saw a naked houri dancing among
 tombstones,
And a babe laughing the while it played
 with skulls.
All this I saw in a dream.
When I waked and looked about me, lo,
 I saw the volcano pouring forth its
 fury,
But I could not hear the blackbird singing.
I saw the heavens scattering snow over the
 hills and valleys,

Garmenting with its white shroud the
        silent lilies.
I saw the graves, row upon row, standing
        before the tranquility of ages, but
        none amongst them dancing of
        praying.
The I beheld hills of skulls, but no
        laughter was there save the laugh
wind.
Waking I saw naught but grief and sorrow.
Where, then, have the joys a dreams departed?
Where hides the splendor of our sleep,
And how has its image vanished?
How can the soul bear patiently until the
        shadow of its yearning shall return
        with sleep?

x x x

Be still, my heart, and attend unto my words.
It was but yesterday that my soul was a tree,
        old and strong,
Whose roots penetrated to the depths of
        the earth and whose branches
        reached toward the infinite,
blooming in spring and bearing
fruit in summer
When autumn was come, I gathered the
fruit on trays of silver and placed
them at the cross-roads,
And the passers-by reached for the fruit
        and ate of it and walked their way.
When autumn was passed and its song was
        turned to wailing and a dirge,
I looked upon my trays and saw that men

had left there but a single fruit;
And when I tasted, I found it bitter as
aloes and sour as a green grape.
Then I said to myself:
"Woe unto me, for I have placed a curse
upon the lips of men, and hostility in
their bowels.
What then, my soul, have you done with
the sweetness that your roots had
sucked from the bosom of earth,
And with fragrance that your boughs had
drunk from the light of the sun?"
Thereupon I uprooted the old and strong
tree of my soul.
I severed it from its past and dismantled
it of the memories of thousand
springs and a thousand autumns.
And I planted the tree of my soul in
another place.
I set it in a field far from the roads of time,
and I passed the night in wakefulness
beside it, giving it to drink of my
tears and my blood, and saying:
"There is a savour in blood, and a sweetness
in tears."
When spring returned, the tree of my soul
bloomed again, and bore fruit in the
summer season.
And when the autumn was come, I gathered
the ripe fruit once more, and I placed
it upon trays of gold at the meeting-
place of the roads.
And men passed by, but no one reached to

take of the fruit.
Then I took and ate, and I found the fruit
as sweet as honey, as luscious as
nectar, perfumed as the breath of
jasmine, and mellow as the wine
of Babylon.
And I cried aloud, saying:
"Men do not desire blessedness upon
their lips, nor truth in their bowels;
For blessedness is the daughter of tears,
and truth is but the son of pain."
Then I returned and sat down under the
shade of the lonely tree of my soul,
and in the field far from the roads
of time.

x x x

Be still, my heart, be still until dawn.
Be still, for space is heavy with the odour
of dead things and cannot inhale
your living breath.
Be still, my heart, and listen to my voice.
It was but yesterday that my thought was
like a ship, rocked upon the waves
of the sea, and moving with the
winds from shore to shore.
And the ship of my thought was empty
save only for seven phials filled to the
brim with seven colours, even the
seven colours of the rainbow.
There came a time when I grew weary of
drifting upon the face of the waters,
and I said:
"I will return with the empty ship of my

thought to the harbor of the town
where I was born."
And as I sailed, I began to paint the sides
of my ship with the seven colour;
And it shone yellow as the sunset, azure
like the sky, and red as a blood-red
anemone;
And upon its sails and rudder I traced
sketches to allure and delight the eye.
And when it was done, the ship of my
thought appeared like the vision of
a prophet
Floating betwixt the two infinities, the sea
And the sky.
Now, when my ship reached port, behold,
All the people came to meet me;
With shout and joy they welcomed me and
They took me into the city,
Beating their tambourines and blowing
Upon their reed flutes.
All this they did because my ship
Appeared enchanting to their eyes;
But none boarded the ship of my thought,
Nor did any perceive that I had brought
My ship empty into port.
Then I said to myself:
"I have misled the people, and with seven
phials of colours have I deceived
their inner and their outer eye."
And when a year was passed, again I
boarded the ship of my thought and
put out to sea.
I sailed to the isles of the East, and there

I gathered myrrh and frankincense
and sandalwood and brought them
to my ship.
I sailed to the isles of the South, and from
thence I brought gold, jade,
and emerald, and every precious stone;
To the isles of the North I sailed, and
found rare silks and velvets and
broideries of every kind;
Thence to the isles of the West and got me
coats of mail, and spears and swords,
and divers weapons.
Thus I filled the ship of my thought with
the costly and strange things of the
earth,
And I turned back to the harbor of my
own city, saying in my heart :
"Now shall my people praise me as a man
worthy of praise.

And now shall they indeed lead me into
the market-place with singing and
piping."
But, behold, when I reached the port, no
man came to meet and welcome me.
Alone I entered the streets of my city, but
no man looked upon me.
Even in the market-squares I stood, telling
of all that I had brought of the
earth's fruit and goodly things.
But the people looked upon me with
Laughter on their faces, and derision
On their lips.

And they turned from me.
Thus was I troubled and cast down, and I turned me to the harbour.
No sooner did my eyes fall upon my ship Than I became aware of a certain Thing to which, in my voyaging
And seeking for good cargoes,
I had paid no heed;
So I cried out in humiliation:
"Behold, the waves of the sea have
Washed the seven colours from my
ship
And now it appears but as a skeleton of bones.
And the winds and the storms and the heat of the sun have effaced from the sails the images of wonder and delight,
And they seem now but as a faded and tattered garment.
Truly I have gathered the earth's costly treasures in a casket floating upon the surface of the waters,
And returned unto my people, but they turn from me.
For their eyes see naught but outward show."
At that very moment I abandoned the ship of my thought and sought the city of the dead,
Where I sat amid the whitened graves and pondered their secrets.
Be still, my heart. Be still until dawn.
Be still, though the tempest mock the

whispering of your depths.
Be still, my heart, until dawn
For whoso awaits the morning patiently,
The morning shall embrace him tenderly.
Behold, my heart, the dawn is come;
Speak, then, if you have yet the power of
    words.
Behold, my heart, the procession of the
    morning.
Did not the silence of the night stir in your
    depths a song wherewith to greet the
    morn?
Behold, the fight of doves and black birds
    above the valley;
Did not the awe of night strength your
    wings to fly with them?
Behold, the shepherds leading their flocks
    from the folds.
Did not the shadows of night urge your
    desire to follow also into the greed
    meadows?
Behold, the young men and the maidens
    hastening towards the vineyard.
Would you not rise and join them?
Arise, my heart. Arise and move with the
    dawn
For night is passed and the fears of night
    have vanished with their black
    dreams.
Arise, my heart, and lift your voice in
    song;
For he who joins not the dawn with his
    singing is but a child of darkness.

Night

O Night, abiding-place of poets and of
            lovers and of singers,
O Night, where shadows dwell with spirits
            and with visions,
O Night, enfolder of our longing, our desire,
            our memory,
Vast giant standing betwixt the dwarfed
            evening clouds and the brides of dawn.
Girt with the sword of awe, crowned with
            The moon, and garmented with silence;
Who gazes with a thousand eyes into the
            depths of life.
And listens with a thousand ears to the
            sighs of desolation and of death!
            ....

It is your darkness that reveals to us the
            light of heaven,
For the light of day has enshrouded us
            with the darkness of earth.
It is your promise that opens our eyes to
            eternity,
For the vanity of day had held us like
            blink men in the world of time and
            space.
It is your tranquil silence that unveils the
            secret of ever wakeful, ever restless spirits;

For day is a turbulent clamour
> wherein souls lie beneath the sharp hooves of
> ambition and desire.

O Night, you are a shepherd who gathers
> unto the fold of sleep the dreams of
> the weak and the hopes of the strong.

You are a seer who closes with his mystic \
> fingers the eyelids of the wretched
> and lifts their hearts to a world more
> kindly than this world.

In the folds of your grey garments lovers
> have found their bower.

And upon your feet, wet with the dew of
> heaven, have the lonely-hearted wept
> their tears;

In the palms of your hands, fragrant with
> the scent of field and vineyard,
> strangers have laid down their
> longing and despair;

To lovers you are a friend; to the lonely,
> a comforter; to the desolate, a host.

In your deep shade the poet's fancies stir;
> on your bosom the prophetic heart
> awakes; upon your brow imagination
> writes.

For to the poet you are a sovereign, to the
> prophet a vision, and to the thinker
> an intimate.

....

When my soul became weary of man, and
> my eyes were tired of gazing upon
> the face of the day.

I sought the distant fields where the shadows
           of bygone ages sleep.
There I stood before a dark and silence being
           moving with a thousand feet over
           the mountain, and over the valley
           and the pain.
There I gazed into the eyes of darkness
           and listened to the murmuring of
           invisible wings.
There I felt the touch of formless garments
           and was shaken by the terrors of the
           unseen.
There I saw you. Night tragic and
           beautiful and awesome,
Standing between the heaven and the
           earth, with clouds for your garment,
           girdled with the fog,
Laughing at the light of the sun and mocking
           the supremacy of the day,
Deriding the multitude of slaves who
           kneel sleepless before their idols,
           and contemptuous of kings who lie
           asleep and dreaming in their beds of silk;
There I beheld you gazing into the eyes of
           thieves, and I beheld you keeping
           guard above the babe in slumber;
I saw you weeping before the smiles of
           prostitutes, and smiling at the tears
           of lovers,
And lifting with your right hand the great-
           hearted, and with your feet trampling
           the mean-spirited.
There I saw you, Night, and you saw me;

You, in your awful beauty, were to me a
      father, and I,
      in my dreams, was a son;
For the curtains of being were drawn
      away, and the veil of doubt was rent;
You revealed your secret purpose unto
      me, and I told you all my hopes and
      my desires.
Then was your majesty turned into melody
      more beautiful than the gentle
      whisper of flowers.
And my fears were transformed into trust
      more than the trust of birds;
And you lifted me and placed me on your
      shoulders.
And you taught my eyes to see, my ears to
      hear, my lips to speak, and my heart
      to love;
With your magic fingers you touched my
      thought.
And my thought poured forth like a
      flowing, singing stream,
      bearing away all
      that was withered grass.
And with your lips you kissed my spirit,
      and it kindled into flames
Devouring every dead and dying thing.

          ....

I followed you, O Night, until I became
      like unto you;
I went as your companion until your
      desires became mine;

I loved you until my whole being was
    indeed a lesser image of your own.
For within my dark self are glowing stars
    which passion scatters at evening and
    doubt gathers at dawn;
And within my heart is a moon that struggles,
    now with thick clouds, and now
    with a procession of dreams that fills
    all space.
Now within my awakened soul dwells
    a peace that reveals the lover's secret
    and the worshiper's prayer;
And upon my head rests a veil of mystery
    which the agony of death my rend,
    but the songs of youth shall weave
    again.
I am like you, O Night, and if men shall
    deem me boastful,
Do they not boast of their resemblance to
    the day?
I am like you, and like you I am accused
    of much that I am not.
I am like you with all my dreams and all
    my hopes and being.
I am like you, even though dusk does not
    crown me with its golden fleece.
I am like you, though morn does not adorn
    my trailing raiment with pearl and
    rose.
I am like you, though I am not yet belted
    with the milky way.
I too am a night, vast and calm, yet
    fettered and rebellious.

There is no beginning to my darkness and
    no end to my depths.
When the souls of the departed rise to
    pride themselves upon the light of
    joy,
My night soul shall descend glorified by
    the darkness of its sorrow.
I am like you, O Night, and when my
    dawn comes, then also shall come my
    end.

In The City Of The Dead

It was but yesterday I escaped the tumult
 of the city
And went forth to walk in the silent fields;
And I came unto a lofty hill
Where nature had bestowed the gift of
 her bountiful hand.
I ascended the hill and looked back upon
 the city.
And lo, the city appeared, with all its
 towers and temples.
To lie beneath a cloud of thick dark smoke
 that rose up from its forges and its
 factories.
As I sat contemplating from afar the
 works of man,
It seemed that most of them are vain and
 futile.
And heartily I turned my mind away from
 all that the sons of Adam have
 wrought,
And looked upon the fields, the seat of
 God's great glory.
And in their midst I beheld a graveyard
 with tombstones of fair marble, and
 with cypress trees.
There, between the city of the living and
 the city of the dead, I sat

And mused upon the endless struggle and
    the ceaseless turbulence in life.
And the enveloping silence and vast
    dignity in death.
On the one side I beheld hope and despair,
    love and hate, riches and poverty,
    belief and unbelief;
And on the other, dust in dust which
    nature intermingles,
Fashioning therefore its world of green
    and growing things that thrive in the
    deep silence of the night.
While thus I pondered, behold, a great
    crowd, marching slowly, caught my
    vision.
And I heard music filling the air with
    dreary tunes.
Before my eyes passed a procession of the
    great and the lowly of mankind,
Walking together in procession at the
    funeral of a man who had been rich and
    powerful,
The dead followed by the living.
And these wept and cried aloud, filling
    the day with their wailing and their lamentations.
Even unto the burial-place.
And here the priests offered up prayers
    and swung their censers,
And the pipers blew mournfully upon
    their pipes.
The orators stood forth with sounding
    words of eulogy,
And the poets, bemoaning with their

studied verses.
Until all had come unto a weary end.
And then the crowd dispersed, revealing a
proud tombstone which the stonecutters
had vied in making.
And many wreaths of flowers, and garlands
woven by deft and skillful
fingers.
Then the procession returned toward the
city, while I sat watching from afar,
and musing.
And now the sun was sinking toward the
west, and the shadows of the rocks
and trees began to lengthen and
discard their raiment of light.
At that moment I looked, and lo, two men
bearing upon their shoulders a coffin
of plain wood;
And after them a woman came in ragged
garments,
A babe at her breast, and at her feet a dog
that looked now to the woman, now
to the wooden casket.
Only these, in the procession at the
funeral of a man who had been poor
and humble-
The wife whose silent tears bespoke her
sorrow,
A baby crying because his mother wept,
and a faithful beast who would
follow also in his dumb grief.
And when these reached the place of
graves,

They lowered the coffin down into a pit in
    the far corner, well removed from the
    lofty marble tombs.
Then they turned back in silence and in
    desolation.
And the dog's eyes looked oftentimes
    toward the last dwelling-place of his
    friend and master,
Until they had disappeared from sight
    behind the trees.
Thereupon I bent my eyes first upon the
    city of the living, and said to myself:
"This is for the rich and powerful men";
Then I looked upon the city of the dead,
    saying:
"And this is for the rich and powerful
    men."
And I cried aloud: "Where, then, is the
    abiding-place of those who are weak
    and poor, O Lord?"
This I said, and gazed up towards the
    heaven of clouds, glorious with the
    golden rays of the great sun.
And I heard voice within me saying. "It
    is there!"

The Poet

An exile am I in this world.
An exile am I and alone, tormented by my
aloneness, which ever direct my
thought to a magic and unknown
realm
And fills my dreams with shadows of a
region distant and unseen.
An exile am I from my kinsmen and my
countrymen, and should I meet one
of them, I would say to myself:
"Who, then, is this one? Where is it I
have known him?
What bond unites me to him, and why do
I draw near to sit beside him?"
An exile am I from myself, and should I
hear my own tongue speak, my ear
finds the voice strange.
Sometimes I look within and behold my
secret self, a hidden self that laughs
and weeps, that dares and fears.
Then my being marvels at my being, and
my spirit questions mine own spirit.
Yet I remain an exile, unknown, lost in the
mist, clothed with the silence.
An exile am I from my body; and when I
pause before a mirror, behold, in my
face is that which my soul has not
conceived and in my eyes that which
my depths do not contain.

When I walk upon the streets of the city,
    the children follow after me,
        shouting:
"Behold the blind man! Let us give him a
    staff to lean upon."
And in haste I flee from them.
If I meet a bevy of maidens, they cleave to
    my garments, singing:
"He is deaf as a rock! Let us fill his ears
    with harmonies of love and passion."
And from them I flee also.
Whenever I approach the middle-aged in
    the market-place, they gather about
    me, crying:
"He is as mute as a tomb! Let us
    straighten his twisted tongue."
And I hasten from in fear.
And if I pass by a company of elders, they
    point their trembling fingers toward
    me, saying:
"He is a madman who has lost his reason
    in the land of the Djinns and Ghouls!"

        ....

An exile am I in this world.
An exile am I, for I have traversed the
    earth both East and West,
Yet I found not my birthplace, no one
    who knew me or had heard my name.
In the morning I awake to find myself
    imprisoned in a darkened cavern
Where vipers threaten from above, and
    every crawling things infests the walls

and ground.
When I seek the outer light, the shadows
of my body march ahead of me-
Whereto I know not, seeking that I do not
understand, grasping that for which
I have no need.
When eventide is come and I return and
lie upon my bed of thorn and feather,
Strange thoughts beguile me, both fear-
some and joyous, and desire
besiege me with their pains and their
delights.
When it is midnight, the shades of bygone
ages fall upon me, and spirit of
forgotten regions visit me and look upon
me.
And I gaze also upon them, and speak to
them and ask of ancient things,
And with kindliness and smiles they
answer me.
But when I would hold them and keep
them, they escape me
And fade as they were but smoke upon
the air.

....

An exile am I in this world.
An exile am I, and no man understands
the language of my soul.
I pace the wilderness and I behold the
rivulets climbing from the depths of
the valley to the mountain top;
Before my eyes the naked trees come into

       bloom and bear their fruit and
          scatter their dead leaves, all in one
          moment.
And before my eyes their boughs fall to
          the lowland and are turned into dark
          serpents.
Ay, strange are my visions, like unto the
          vision of no man.
For I see birds lifting their wings unto the
          morning with songs, and with
          lamentation;
I see them alight and change before my
          eyes into nude women with long,
          loosened hair.
Who gaze at me from behind eyelids
          painted for love, and who smile upon
          me with lips dipped in honey,
And who stretch white hands to me,
          perfumed with frankincense and myrrh.
And even as I gaze, they vanish like a
          shaken mist.
Leaving in space the echo of their
          mocking laughter.

....

An exile am I in this world.
A poet am I who gathers in verse what life
          scatters in prose;
And scatters in prose what life gathers in
          verse.
And hence an exile am I, and an exile I
          shall remain until death lifts me up
          and bears me even unto my country.

Fame

I walked upon the sand at ebb-tide.
And bending down, I wrote a line upon the sand.
And in that line I wrote what my mind thought
And what my soul desired.
And when the tide was high,
I returned to that very shore,
And of that which I had written I found naught.
I found only the staff-marks of one who had walked blindly.

Earth

With might and power earth springs forth
 out of earth;
Then earth moves over earth with dignity
 and pride;
And earth from earth builds palaces for
 kings,
And lofty towers and goodly temples for
 all people,
And weaves strange myths, strict laws,
 and subtle dogmas.
When all these things are done, earth
 wearies of earth's labour,
And from its light and darkness it creates
 grey shadows, and soft drowsy
 fancies, and enchanting dreams.
Earth's slumber then beguiles earth's
 heavy eyelids,
And they close upon all things in deep and
 quiet slumber.
And earth calls out unto earth, saying:
"Behold, a womb am I, and I am a tomb;
A womb and a tomb I shall remain forever,
Ay, even until the stars are no more,
And until the suns are turned into dead
 ashes."

Kahlil Gibran Biography

Jubran Kahlil Jubran was born on 6 January 1883 to Kamila Jubran and her second husband, Kahlil Sa'd Jubran, in the village of Bisharri in what is now northern Lebanon but was then Ottoman, Syria. He had a half-brother, Butrus (also known as Peter) Rahma, and two younger sisters, Sultana and Marianna. The family were Maronite Christians, and Kamila Jubran was the daughter of a Maronite priest. The father seems to have been a violent drinker and a gambler. Gibran later described his father to his women friends as a descendant of cavaliers, a romantic figure, who got into trouble with the law for refusing to compromise with corrupt village authorities.

Similarly, Gibran later portrayed his life in Lebanon as idyllic, stressing his precocious artistic and literary talents and his mother's efforts to educate him; some of these stories were obviously tall tales meant to impress his American patrons. A local doctor, Salim Dahir, seems to have played a role in Gibran's education. He claimed that his interest in art was inspired in part by a book of Leonardo da Vinci's drawings that his mother gave him. He absorbed a good deal of Lebanese folk culture that appears in his writings.

Kamila left her husband in 1895 and took the children to the United States; they were part of the large wave of immigration that took place in the three decades before World War I. They arrived in New York on 17 June and went on to Boston, where they settled in the teeming immigrant slums of the South End. Kamila, as was common for immigrants, became a peddler; soon she had saved enough money to open a shop with her son Butrus. Kahlil went to school, while his sisters helped in the shop. The school gave him the American form and spelling of his last name, Gibran.

In November 1896 Gibran was introduced to Fred Holland Day, the eccentric leader of a Boston avant-garde group who called themselves the Visionists. They were imitators of the British decadents and Pre-Raphaelites; though their artistic achievements did not equal those of their British models, they established two of the first "little magazines" of poetry and art in America and a distinguished art press, Copeland and Day, that published a hundred highly regarded volumes in five years. Day read to him from English literature and, as Gibran's English improved, lent him books and directed him to the new Boston Public Library. At an exhibit of Day's photographs in 1898 Gibran met a Cambridge poet, Josephine Prescott Peabody who sketched a portrait of her from memory and gave it to Day to pass on to her. Peabody was charmed by the sketch, and she and Gibran exchanged a few letters.

Shortly afterward, Gibran's mother sent him back to Lebanon to continue his education. He attended the Maronite high school Madrasat al-Hikma in Beirut, where he was allowed to study independently; he read widely in Arabic and French literature, started a school poetry magazine, and won a poetry contest. He visited Bisharri during vacations, but his relationship with his father was strained. Several of Gibran's works of fiction—including the novella al-Ajniha al-mutakassira (1912; translated as The Broken Wings, 1957), with its story of a doomed love affair—are set in Beirut and other parts of Lebanon around this time. Gibran left Beirut in 1901 and wandered around Europe; Paris was among the places he visited.

In November 1902 Gibran wrote to Peabody, and she invited him to a party held at her house two weeks later. An intense platonic relationship resulted, though Gibran seems to have wanted it to progress to a sexual one. He visited her regularly; they went to musical and artistic events together; they wrote to each other often; and she encouraged his writing and his art. She gave him the nickname that he later used as the title of his most famous book: "the Prophet." The relationship must have been a comfort to Gibran during the harrowing months when his brother and mother were dying. In May, Peabody helped to arrange to have Gibran's work included in an art exhibition at Wellesley College. Kamila died on 28 June, leaving Gibran responsible for Marianna and the debt-ridden family shop. He ran the business long enough to pay off the debts, then allowed Marianna to support the two of them on her earnings as a seamstress. In October 1903 Gibran wrote something in a letter to Peabody that angered her, and their relationship cooled.

In April 1904 Day held an exhibit of Gibran's work at his studio. It was favorably reviewed, and some of the pictures were sold. At the show Gibran met a woman who became his most important patron, Mary Haskelwho was from a wealthy South Carolina family and ran a private Boston girls' school. Unlike Peabody and the other women who drifted in and out of Gibran's life, she was a hardheaded businesswoman. She recorded their conversations and preserved his sketches and other ephemera in extremely detailed journals. She supported him intellectually, financially, and emotionally.

Day's studio burned in the winter of 1904, destroying Gibran's entire portfolio. Around that time Ameen Guraieb, the editor of the New York Arabic newspaper al-Mohajer (The Emigrant), hired Gibran to write a weekly column. In 1905 Guraieb published Gibran's first book, al-Musiqa (On Music). By 1906 Gibran's columns in al-Mohajer, which had come to be titled "Dam'a wa'btisama" (Tears and Laughter), were becoming popular because of their difference from conventional Arabic literature. Arabic writers were expected to have mastered the rigid poetic forms and vocabulary of the pre-Islamic period and the first centuries of Islam; having absorbed this rich literary heritage, they could not escape its overwhelming influence. Gibran, however, did not have the training to imitate the old masters of Arabic literature: his education had been haphazard and was as much in English as in Arabic, and there is little evidence of the influence of classical Arabic literature in his works. Instead, his Arabic style was influenced by the Romantic writers of late 19th-century Europe and shows obvious traces of English syntax.

In 1906 Gibran published 'Ara'is al-muruj (Spirit Brides; translated as Nymphs of the Valley, 1948), a collection of three short stories. "Rimal al-ajyal wa al-nar al-khalidah" (The Ash of Centuries and the Immortal Flame) is a story of reincarnation. Nathan, the son of the priest of Astarte in Baalbek, loses his lover to disease. During this period Haskell introduced him to an aspiring French actress, Émilie Michel, who taught French at Haskell's school, and the two fell in love. In 1908 Michel suffered an ectopic pregnancy and had an abortion.

Gibran's al-Arwah al-mutamarrida (translated as Spirits Rebellious, 1948), a collection of four stories, appeared in 1908. In 1908 Haskell paid for Gibran travel to Paris to study art. There he improved his skill with pastels and oils and was impressed by the symbolist paintings of Eugene Carrière. In Paris he also encountered the works of the German philosopher Friedrich Nietzsche, who became a major influence on his writing. He met several Syrian political exiles and the Lebanese American writer Amin Rihani, who became his friend and literary ally. Eventually his money ran out, and he returned to the United States in October 1910.

After Paris, Gibran found Boston provincial and stifling. Haskell arranged for him to visit New York in April 1911. New York was the center of the Arabic literary scene in America; Rihani was there, and Gibran met many literary and artistic figures who lived in or passed through the city, including the Irish poet and dramatist William Butler Yeats. He grew more politically active, supporting the idea of revolution to gain Syrian independence from the Ottoman Empire.

Gibran's literary career, however, was blossoming. Al-Funun (The Arts), an Arabic newspaper founded in New York in 1913, provided a new vehicle for his writings, some of which were openly political. The editor of al-Funun published a collection of fifty-six of Gibran's early newspaper columns as Dam'a wa ibtisamah (1914; translated as A Tear and a Smile, 1950); most are a page or two long, and the volume as a whole comprises about a hundred pages

During World War I, Gibran was active in Syrian nationalist circles and in efforts to bring relief to the starving people of his homeland. Gibran's first book in English, *The Madman: His Parables and Poems*, was completed in 1917; it was brought out in 1918 by the young literary publisher Alfred A. Knopf, who went on to publish all of Gibran's English works. In 1919 Gibran published al-Mawakib (translated as The Procession, 1947). A fourth collection of Gibran's Arabic stories and prose poems, al-'Awasif (The Storms), came out in Cairo in 1920. Also in 1920 Knopf published *The Forerunner: His Parables and Poems*.

Al-Bada'i' wa al-tara'if (Best Things and Masterpieces), a collection of thirty-five of Gibran's pieces, was published in Cairo in 1923. Gibran's masterpiece, *The Prophet*, was published in September 1923. The earliest references to a mysterious prophet counseling his people before returning to his island home can be found in Haskell's journal from 1912. The Prophet received tepid reviews in *Poetry and The Bookman*, an enthusiastic review in the Chicago Evening Post, and little else. On the other hand, the public reception was intense. The last of Gibran's Arabic books was published in 1929. *Al-Sanabil (Heads of Grain)* is a commemorative anthology of his works that was presented to him at an Arrabitah banquet. Gibran's final work to be published in his lifetime was *The Earth Gods (1931)*. Around the end of March 1931 Gibran sent the manuscript for *The Wanderer: His Parables and His Sayings*

(1932) to Haskell for editing. The form of the work is that of *The Madman* and *The Forerunner*. At his death Gibran was working on *The Garden of the Prophet* (1933), which was to be the second volume in a trilogy begun by *The Prophet*. It is the story of Almustafa's return to his native island and deals with humanity's relationship with nature. Of the third volume, "The Death of the Prophet," only one sentence was written: "And he shall return to the City of Orphalese ... and they shall stone him in the marketplace, even unto death; and he shall call every stone a blessed name."

Gibran died on 10 April 1931 of cirrhosis of the liver. He was an alcoholic and had been in poor health since the early 1920s. His body was taken to Boston, and despite his family's fears that he would be denied Catholic rites, his friend Monsignor Stephen El-Douaihy conducted a funeral mass. Hundreds attended—far too many for all of them to get into the church. Gibran's death set off a series of sordid conflicts that have clouded his reputation. His will left money and real estate to his sister (Marianna Jubran never married and died in Boston in 1972) and his papers and the contents of his studio to Haskell, with a request that she send any materials she did not want to Bisharri; he also left the royalties from his copyrights to the village. At the studio Haskell found her own correspondence with Gibran, his other correspondence, her notebooks, and Gibran's manuscripts; she locked them in two large suitcases and sealed the studio. Haskell, however, had to return to her husband and relied on Young to handle affairs in New York. Young was immediately jealous of Haskell, whose existence she had only discovered after Gibran's death. She wanted to destroy Gibran's letters, especially the correspondence with Haskell; while Haskell was able to prevent her from doing so, Young did destroy or return letters from others. There is little question that she was trying to protect Gibran's reputation from any taint of normal humanity.

The most serious problem concerned Young's handling of

Gibran's unpublished manuscripts. Haskell had finished editing *The Wanderer* after Gibran's death and sent it to Young, who undid the editing and published it with the original "words of the blessed one." The infuriated Haskell demanded that all of the English manuscripts be sent to her immediately. When they arrived, those for *The Wanderer and The Garden of the Prophet* were missing. Young explained that she had destroyed the manuscript for *The Wanderer* that Haskell had edited; as for *The Garden of the Prophet*, she later wrote that the urge to complete the book came to her "in the deep of night" and that "his glowing words came into being as if he were indeed supplying the need." Finally, her 1945 biography of Gibran, an adulatory work full of misinformation — much of which may have come from Gibran himself — continues to create confusion even after the publication of several excellent biographies.

The other major difficulty concerned Gibran's bequest of his royalties to his native village. By the time the copyrights came up for renewal, sales of Gibran's works were substantial; his sister contested the will, which was not properly drafted. The village won, but at the cost of giving 25 percent of the royalties to its lawyer and, later, his heirs. The unearned wealth wrought havoc in Bisharri, dividing families and leading to at least two murders. The Lebanese government finally had to step in to restore peace and deal with the corruption that was dissipating the funds. The feud among the copyright holders has prevented the publication of Haskell's journals, creating an impediment to Gibran studies. The journals are also a literary loss in themselves.

Kahlil Gibran occupies an enquiring place in literary history. As one of the writers who broke with the old and rigid conventions of Arabic poetry and literary prose, he is among the great figures in the twentieth-century revival of Arabic literature. His Arabic works are read, admired, and taught, and they are published and sold among the classics of Arabic literature. In English, on the other hand, a chasm remains between his popularity and the lack of critical respect for his work. Although in the 1910s his writings were published by Knopf alongside those of such authors as Eliot and Frost, he quickly ceased to be considered an important writer by critics. He has generally been dismissed as sentimental and mawkishly mystical. Nevertheless, his works are widely read and are regarded as serious literature by people who do not often read such literature. The unconventional beauty of his language and the moral earnestness of his ideas allow him to speak to a broad audience as only a handful of other n published. His literary and artistic models were the Romantics of the late nineteenth century to whom he was introduced as a teenager by his avant-garde friends in Boston, and Gibran's continuing popularity as a writer testifies to the lasting power of the Romantic practice in world literature.

Black Eagle Books

www.blackeaglebooks.org
info@blackeaglebooks.org

Black Eagle Books, an independent publisher, was founded as a nonprofit organization in April, 2019. It is our mission to connect and engage the Indian diaspora and the world at large with the best of works of world literature published on a collaborative platform, with special emphasis on foregrounding Contemporary Classics and New Writing.

www.ingramcontent.com/pod-product-compliance
Lightning Source LLC
Chambersburg PA
CBHW020524080526
44583CB00013B/722